The Green 101 Meatless Recipes

The Delightful Dine-In Amem

Copyright © 2023 The Delightful Dine-In Amem
All rights reserved.
:

Contents

INTRODUCTION 7
1. Vegan Pulled BBQ Jackfruit Sandwich 9
2. Smoky Maple Bacon Tempeh 10
3. Buffalo Cauliflower Wings 11
4. Seitan Pepperoni Pizza 12
5. BBQ "Ribs" with Tangy Sauce 13
6. Herbivorous Burger with Vegan Cheese 14
7. Coconut Curry Tofu 15
8. Vegan "Chicken" and Waffles 16
9. Spicy Black Bean Burger 18
10. Sweet and Sour Tempeh Stir Fry 18
11. Jackfruit Carnitas Tacos 20
12. Tempeh Bacon Breakfast Burrito 21
13. BBQ "Chick'n" Salad 22
14. Vegan "Beef" and Broccoli Stir Fry 22
15. Chickpea Tuna Salad Sandwich 23
16. Vegan Sausage and Peppers 24
17. BBQ "Chick'n" Skewers 25
18. Buffalo Chickpea Salad 26
19. Mushroom and Spinach Stuffed Shells 27
20. Teriyaki Tofu Stir Fry 28
21. Vegan "Chicken" Parmesan 29
22. Spicy Sriracha Tofu 31
23. Vegan "Meatball" Sub 31
24. BBQ Cauliflower Bites 32
25. Seitan Philly Cheesesteak 33
26. Coconut Curry Chickpea Stew 34
27. Vegan Breakfast Sausage Patties 36

28. Vegan "Beef" Fajitas 37
29. Smoky Chipotle Tempeh Tacos 38
30. Jackfruit Crab Cakes 39
31. Tempeh Bacon BLT Sandwich 40
32. Vegan "Chicken" Enchiladas 41
33. Korean BBQ Tofu Lettuce Wraps 42
34. BBQ "Chick'n" Pizza 43
35. Vegan Sloppy Joes 44
36. Chickpea and Vegetable Curry 45
37. Vegan "Meatball" Spaghetti 46
38. Buffalo Cauliflower Salad 47
39. Teriyaki Tofu Noodle Bowl 48
40. Vegan "Beef" Stir Fry 49
41. Seitan Gyro Wrap 50
42. BBQ Jackfruit Sliders 51
43. Spicy Buffalo Tofu Nuggets 52
44. Vegan Breakfast Burrito Bowl 53
45. Chickpea Shawarma Wrap 54
46. Vegan "Chicken" Caesar Salad 55
47. Coconut Curry Lentil Soup 56
48. Vegan Sausage Breakfast Skillet 57
49. Vegan "Beef" Tacos 57
50. Jackfruit Banh Mi Sandwich 59
51. Tempeh Bacon and Avocado Wrap 60
52. BBQ "Chick'n" Quesadillas 60
53. Buffalo Cauliflower Wrap 61
54. Teriyaki Tofu Rice Bowl 62
55. Vegan "Meatball" Stroganoff 63
56. Smoky Chipotle Seitan Tacos 64

57. Vegan "Chicken" and Waffle Sliders 66
58. Spicy Buffalo Chickpea Salad 67
59. Vegan Gyro Bowl 68
60. BBQ Jackfruit Nachos 69
61. Vegan Breakfast Hash 70
62. Chickpea and Vegetable Stir Fry 71
63. Vegan "Beef" and Black Bean Burritos 72
64. Jackfruit Curry 73
65. Tempeh Bacon Breakfast Sandwich 74
66. BBQ "Chick'n" Lettuce Wraps 75
67. Buffalo Cauliflower Mac and Cheese 76
68. Teriyaki Tofu and Vegetable Skewers 77
69. Vegan "Meatball" Sub Salad 78
70. Smoky Chipotle Tempeh Wrap 79
71. Vegan "Chicken" Fried Rice 80
72. Coconut Curry Quinoa Salad 82
73. Vegan Sausage and Spinach Stuffed Portobello Mushrooms 83
74. BBQ Jackfruit Stuffed Sweet Potatoes 84
75. Buffalo Cauliflower Tacos 86
76. Teriyaki Tofu Noodle Stir Fry 87
77. Vegan "Beef" and Mushroom Pot Pie 88
78. Jackfruit Tostadas 89
79. Tempeh Bacon and Egg Breakfast Burrito 90
80. BBQ "Chick'n" Lettuce Cups 91
81. Spicy Buffalo Chickpea Wraps 92
82. Vegan Gyro Pita Pockets 93
83. Vegan "Meatball" Stuffed Bell Peppers 94
84. Smoky Chipotle Seitan Burger 95
85. Coconut Curry Lentil Buddha Bowl 96

86. Vegan Sausage Breakfast Tacos 98
87. Vegan "Beef" and Quinoa Stuffed Bell Peppers 99
88. Jackfruit Chili 100
89. Teriyaki Tofu and Broccoli Stir Fry 101
90. BBQ "Chick'n" Flatbread 102
91. Buffalo Cauliflower Salad Bowl 103
92. Tempeh Bacon and Avocado Toast 104
93. Vegan "Chicken" Pad Thai 105
94. Chickpea and Vegetable Coconut Curry 106
95. Vegan "Meatball" and Veggie Skewers 108
96. Smoky Chipotle Tempeh Lettuce Wraps 109
97. BBQ Jackfruit Baked Potatoes 110
98. Teriyaki Tofu Sushi Rolls 111
99. Vegan "Beef" and Potato Curry 112
100. Jackfruit BBQ Sliders 113
101. Tempeh Bacon and Spinach Salad 114
CONCLUSION 116

INTRODUCTION

When it comes to living a healthier lifestyle, adding more plant-based meals to your diet can be an important part of achieving that goal. The Green Butcher: 101 Meatless Recipes provides an excellent guide to delicious plant-based recipes that are both easy and nutritious to prepare. The recipes in this cookbook draw inspiration from around the world and range from vegan classics to dishes that are entirely unique and unexpected.

The Green Butcher will provide you with all the information and tools you need to create delicious and flavorful meat-free dishes. All of the recipes in this cookbook focus on natural unprocessed ingredients including fruits, vegetables, grains, legumes, nuts, and seeds. This book also explains the various benefits of a vegan diet as well as tips on how to create an appealing and balanced vegan plate.

The book begins with a helpful guide on how to stock your pantry and fridge with the necessary ingredients to prepare fantastic vegan meals. You will then learn about the basics of the vegan cooking and how to prepare the most popular vegan dishes. After that, you will be introduced to 101 delicious meat-free recipes that are sure to please even the most discerning of eaters.

The recipes range from savory to sweet dishes, all of which feature a variety of vegetables, fruits, legumes, grains, nuts, and seeds as primary ingredients. You will find breakfast recipes such as Baked Oatmeal with Nuts and Fruits, dinner recipes like Chickpea Biryani, and even vegan versions of popular comfort food such as Enchiladas Verdes. There are also several desserts and snacks to choose from, such as Salted Dark Chocolate Brownies and Ice Cream Sandwich Cookies.

Each recipe in The Green Butcher includes a list of necessary ingredients, detailed instructions, preparation time, and a note about its nutritional content. There are also helpful photos for each recipe to help you perfectly replicate the dish. Additionally, the book includes several meal plans for those following a vegan diet, such as an 8-week weight loss plan or a 7-day vegan cleanse.

Whether you are taking the first steps in exploring the vegan lifestyle, want to add more variety to your vegan diet, or just enjoy trying new recipes, The Green Butcher: 101 Meatless Recipes will prove to be an invaluable guide. With this cookbook, you will learn new cooking techniques, broaden your flavor palette, and discover creative and delicious dishes that are completely plant-based.

1. Vegan Pulled BBQ Jackfruit Sandwich

This vegan pulled BBQ jackfruit sandwich is the perfect combination of flavor, texture, and nutrition. It's easy to make, delicious, and great for sharing!
Serving: 4 servings
Preparation Time: 10 minutes
Ready Time: 45 minutes

Ingredients:
- 2 20-ounce cans young green jackfruit, preferably in brine or water
- 2 tablespoons olive oil
- 1 onion, diced
- 2 cloves garlic, minced
- 1/4 cup vegetable broth or water
- 1/2 teaspoon chili powder
- 1/4 teaspoon smoked paprika
- 2 tablespoons vegan Worcestershire sauce
- 2 tablespoons tomato paste
- 2 tablespoons apple cider vinegar
- 1/4 cup barbecue sauce, plus more for Serving: • 4 whole wheat buns
- Chopped cilantro, for garnish

Instructions:
1. Preheat oven to 375°F (190°C). Drain jackfruit and pat dry.
2. Heat olive oil in a large skillet over medium-high heat. Add onion and garlic and cook, stirring occasionally, until the onion is softened, about 5 minutes.
3. Add jackfruit and vegetable broth. Use a spoon or spatula to break up the jackfruit into shreds.
4. Add chili powder, smoked paprika, vegan Worcestershire sauce, tomato paste, and apple cider vinegar. Stir to combine. Simmer for 15 minutes, stirring occasionally.
5. Add barbecue sauce and stir to combine. Transfer the mixture to a greased baking dish.
6. Bake for 30 minutes, or until the jackfruit is tender.
7. Toast the buns if desired. Serve the jackfruit on the buns with extra barbecue sauce and cilantro for garnish, if desired.

Nutrition information: Per Serving: 212 calories; 6.6 g fat; 28.7 g carbohydrates; 5.3 g protein; 3.5 g fiber; 178 mg sodium.

2. Smoky Maple Bacon Tempeh

This smoky maple bacon tempeh dish is a savoury and delicious vegan dinner that is simple to prepare and requires minimal Ingredients.
Serving: 5
Preparation Time: 10 minutes
Ready Time: 25 minutes

Ingredients:
- 2 8 oz. packages of tempeh
- 2 tablespoons of olive oil
- 2 tablespoons of smoked paprika
- 2 tablespoons of maple syrup
- 2 tablespoons of soy sauce
- 2 cloves of garlic, minced
- 1/2 teaspoon of black pepper

Instructions:
1. Preheat oven to 375 degrees F.
2. Slice the tempeh into thin strips and set aside.
3. In a bowl, mix together the olive oil, smoked paprika, maple syrup, soy sauce, garlic and black pepper, until fully combined.
4. Use a brush or a spoon to evenly spread the marinade over each tempeh strip.
5. Place the tempeh strips onto a parchment-lined baking sheet, and bake for 25 minutes until golden.
6. Serve hot and enjoy!

Nutrition information:
Per Serving:
Calories: 196
Fat: 7g
Carbohydrates: 12g
Protein: 19g

3. Buffalo Cauliflower Wings

Buffalo cauliflower wings are a tasty low-carb alternative to traditional chicken wings. This scrumptious dish is simple to make and can be served as a side dish or main meal.
Serving: 4
Preparation time: 10 minutes
Ready time: 20 minutes

Ingredients:
- 1 head of cauliflower, cut into florets
- 2 tablespoons all-purpose flour
- 1/2 cup water
- 1/2 teaspoon garlic powder
- 1/4 teaspoon paprika
- 1/2 teaspoon cayenne pepper
- 3/4 cup hot sauce, plus more to taste
- 1/4 cup melted butter
- Salt and pepper, to taste

Instructions:
1. Preheat oven to 450°F (230°C).
2. In a shallow bowl, combine flour and water to make a thick batter. Add garlic powder, paprika and cayenne pepper and mix until fully combined.
3. Dip the cauliflower florets into the batter, then arrange on a baking sheet lined with parchment paper.
4. Bake for 15 minutes, or until golden brown.
5. Meanwhile, mix together the hot sauce and melted butter in a medium-sized bowl.
6. Remove the cauliflower from the oven and add to the bowl with the hot sauce and butter mixture. Toss until evenly coated.
7. Spread the buffalo cauliflower back onto the baking sheet and bake for an additional 5 minutes.
8. Remove from oven and season with salt, pepper, and extra hot sauce, if desired.

Nutrition information:
Calories: 108 kcal, Carbohydrates: 9.3 g, Protein: 4.2 g, Fat: 6.5 g, Saturated Fat: 4 g, Sodium: 1,547 mg, Fiber: 1.6 g, Sugar: 3 g

4. Seitan Pepperoni Pizza

Take a chance on this unique and delicious vegan spin on traditional pepperoni pizza. Seitan Pepperoni Pizza is a flavorful, gluten-free pizza with a crispy, cheesy crust. It's sure to satisfy all the pizza lovers in your life!
Serving: 4
Preparation time: 25 mins
Ready time: 45 mins

Ingredients:
- 1 recipe Seitan Pepperoni
- 3-4 cups pizza sauce
- 20 oz vegan mozzarella cheese, shredded
- 2 cups vegan Parmesan cheese, shredded
- 2 1/2 cups gluten-free pizza crust mix
- Olive oil
- 1/4 cup vegan butter, melted
- 1/2 teaspoon garlic powder

Instructions:
1. Preheat oven to 375°F.
2. Prepare the Seitan Pepperoni according to recipe instructions.
3. In a mixing bowl, whisk together the gluten-free pizza crust mix with the melted vegan butter and garlic powder.
4. Grease a large baking sheet with olive oil.
5. Spread the pizza dough onto the baking sheet and pre-bake for 18-20 minutes.
6. Remove from the oven and spread the pizza sauce evenly over the crust.
7. Top with mozzarella and Parmesan cheese.
8. Place the Seitan Pepperoni slices on top.
9. Bake for an additional 20-25 minutes or until cheese is melted.
10. Slice and serve pizza hot.

Nutrition information:
Serving: 1 slice | Calories: 361 kcal | Carbohydrates: 24.6 g | Protein: 21.9 g | Fat: 18.3 g | Saturated Fat: 7.1 g | Sodium: 905 mg | Potassium: 451 mg | Fiber: 3.6 g | Sugar: 4.4 g | Calcium: 240 mg | Iron: 2.1 mg

5. BBQ "Ribs" with Tangy Sauce

BBQ Ribs with Tangy Sauce is a wonderfully flavorful, yet simple recipe that is sure to be a crowd-pleaser. Succulent pork ribs are baked until tender and then finished on the grill with a tangy sauce for a delicious and memorable meal.
Serving: 12 servings
Preparation Time: 15 minutes
Ready Time: 3 hours

Ingredients:
- 2 racks of baby back pork ribs
- 2 tablespoons of garlic powder
- 2 tablespoons of smoked paprika
- 1 tablespoon of onion powder
- 2 teaspoons of chili powder
- ½ teaspoon of black pepper
- ½ teaspoon of ground marjoram
- ½ teaspoon of ground thyme
- ½ teaspoon of cumin
- For the Sauce:
- 2 tablespoons of apple cider vinegar
- 2 tablespoons of honey
- ¼ cup of ketchup
- 2 tablespoons of Worcestershire sauce
- 2 tablespoons of tomato paste
- 2 tablespoons of Dijon mustard
- ½ teaspoon of ground black pepper

Instructions:
1. Preheat the oven to 225 degrees Fahrenheit.

2. Rinse the ribs and pat dry. Cut the racks of ribs into sections that will fit in baking dish.
3. In a small bowl, mix together garlic powder, smoked paprika, onion powder, chili powder, black pepper, ground marjoram, ground thyme, and cumin. Get a generous amount of the spice mix on each section of ribs, massaging the spices into the meat.
4. Place the sections of ribs onto a baking sheet lined with parchment paper (this will help prevent sticking). Cover with foil and seal tightly around the edges. Bake for 2 hours.
5. In the meantime, prepare the sauce by combining apple cider vinegar, honey, ketchup, Worcestershire sauce, tomato paste, Dijon mustard, and black pepper into a saucepan. Bring to a boil, then reduce the heat and simmer for 8-10 minutes.
6. Preheat the grill to medium-high heat.
7. When the ribs have finished baking, brush with the prepared sauce all over both sides of the ribs. Place them onto the preheated grill and cook for 4-5 minutes per side until the sauce is caramelized and lightly charred.

Nutrition information:
- Calories: 259 kcal
- Carbohydrates: 21.1g
- Protein: 10.6g
- Fat:15.6g
- Saturated Fat:5.9g
- Cholesterol:32mg
- Sodium:527mg
- Potassium:315mg
- Fiber:0.9g
- Sugar:16.4g
- Vitamin A:372IU
- Vitamin C:1.2mg
- Calcium:31mg
- Iron:1.7mg

6. Herbivorous Burger with Vegan Cheese

This Herbivorous Burger with Vegan Cheese is a delicious and nutritious vegan meal. Serve it up for lunch or dinner and enjoy! Serving: 4
Preparation time: 10 minutes Ready time: 10 minutes

Ingredients:
- 1 16-ounce package of vegan burger patties
- 1 avocado
- 6 slices vegan cheese
- 4 hamburger buns
- 1 tomato, sliced
- 1/2 red onion, sliced
- 1/4 cup vegan mayonnaise
- Salt and pepper to taste

Instructions:
1. Preheat the oven to 350°F.
2. Place vegan burger patties on a baking sheet and bake for 10-12 minutes.
3. Meanwhile, in a small bowl, mash the avocado with a fork. Add a pinch of salt and pepper.
4. Toast the hamburger buns.
5. Place the vegan burger patty onto each bun.
6. Top with a slice of vegan cheese, the mashed avocado, tomato, onion, and vegan mayonnaise.
7. Enjoy!

Nutrition information (per serving):
- Calories: 519
- Fat: 23g
- Cholesterol: 0mg
- Sodium: 828mg
- Carbs: 44g
- Sugar: 4g
- Fiber: 8g
- Protein: 28g

7. Coconut Curry Tofu

Coconut Curry Tofu is a simple, healthy, vegan recipe. It combines flavorful curry spices, creamy coconut milk, and hearty tofu to make a delicious and warming meal that can be ready in about 30 minutes.
Serving: This Coconut Curry Tofu recipe serves 2.
Preparation Time: This recipe takes 10 minutes to prepare.
Ready Time: This recipe takes 20 minutes to cook.

Ingredients:
- 1 block (14 ounces) firm or extra-firm tofu, pressed and cubed
- 1 tablespoon cooking oil
- 2 tablespoons madras curry powder
- 1 teaspoon ground turmeric
- 1 can (14 ounces) light coconut milk
- 2 to 3 tablespoons tamari or soy sauce
- 1 large tomato, diced
- 1 red or green bell pepper, diced
- 1/4 cup fresh cilantro leaves

Instructions:
1. Heat the oil in a large skillet over medium heat.
2. Add the tofu cubes and cook until lightly browned, stirring occasionally.
3. Reduce the heat to low and add the curry powder, turmeric, and coconut milk. Simmer for 10 minutes.
4. Add the tamari or soy sauce, diced tomato, bell pepper, and cilantro. Simmer for an additional 10 minutes.

Nutrition information:
Per Serving: 350 calories; 18g fat; 17g carbohydrates; 20g protein

8. Vegan "Chicken" and Waffles

This Vegan "Chicken" and Waffles will make your mouth water with its delightfully crunchy exterior and savory flavors. Not only is this dish vegan-friendly, but is also incredibly easy to make.
Serving: 3-4
Preparation Time: 10 minutes
Ready time: 20 minutes

Ingredients:
- 1/2 cup vegan buttery spread
- 2 cups unsweetened almond milk
- 1 teaspoon granulated sugar
- 1 teaspoon garlic powder
- 1 teaspoon onion powder
- 1/2 teaspoon nutritional yeast
- 2 cups all-purpose flour
- 2 teaspoons baking powder
- 1 teaspoon kosher salt
- 2 tablespoons vegan buttery spread, melted
- 2 cups vegan chicken-style strips
- 2 cups vegetable oil, for frying

Instructions:
1. Preheat the oven to 375° F.
2. In a medium bowl, whisk together the vegan buttery spread, almond milk, sugar, garlic powder, onion powder, and nutritional yeast until fully combined.
3. In a large bowl, whisk together the flour, baking powder, and salt. Gradually add the almond milk mixture, stirring until just combined.
4. Heat the oil in a large skillet over medium-high heat.
5. Dip each vegan chicken-style strip in the batter and add to the hot oil. Fry for 3-4 minutes per side, or until golden-brown.
6. Transfer the fried vegan chicken-style strips to a baking sheet lined with parchment paper.
7. Bake for 15-20 minutes, or until the vegan chicken-style strips are cooked through.
8. Serve the strips over a bed of warm vegan waffles.

Nutrition information:
Per serving:
Calories: 325 kcal, Protein: 6.3 g, Total Fat: 13.2 g, Saturated Fat: 4.5 g, Carbohydrates: 42 g, Dietary Fiber: 1.7 g, Sugars: 5.8 g, Sodium: 602.2 mg.

9. Spicy Black Bean Burger

This spicy black bean burger is a flavorful and healthy meal. It's both vegan and gluten-free, and can be served with almost any side dish.
Serving: Serves 4
Preparation time: 20 minutes
Ready time: 40 minutes

Ingredients:
- 2 cans black beans, drained and rinsed
- 1/2 cup oats
- 1/4 cup diced red onion
- 2 cloves garlic, minced
- 1/4 teaspoon ground cumin
- 2 teaspoons chili powder
- Salt and pepper to taste
- 2 tablespoons vegetable oil

Instructions:
1. In a large bowl, mash the beans until mostly smooth.
2. Mix in the oats, red onion, garlic, cumin, chili powder, salt, and pepper until evenly combined.
3. Form into four patties.
4. Heat the oil in a large skillet over medium-high heat.
5. Add the patties to the skillet and cook until crispy and browned on both sides, about 5 minutes per side.
6. Serve with your favorite toppings and sides.

Nutrition information: Per Serving: 260 calories, 9 g fat, 30 g carbohydrates, 11 g protein, 11 g fiber, 160 mg sodium.

10. Sweet and Sour Tempeh Stir Fry

Sweet and Sour Tempeh Stir Fry is an easy and delicious meal that combines savory and tangy flavors into an enjoyable dish. It is perfect for a weeknight dinner or as a side dish.
Serving: Serves 4
Preparation Time: 10 minutes

Ready Time: 20 minutes

Ingredients:
- 2 tablespoons olive oil
- 1 package tempeh, cubed
- 1 small onion, diced
- 1 green bell pepper, diced
- 2 tablespoons freshly grated ginger
- 2 cloves garlic, minced
- 2 tablespoons tomato paste
- 1/4 cup rice vinegar
- 2 tablespoons honey
- 2 tablespoons soy sauce
- 2 tablespoons cornstarch
- 1/4 cup water
- 1/4 cup roasted peanuts, chopped

Instructions:
1. Heat the oil in a large skillet over medium heat. Add the tempeh and cook, stirring frequently, for about 5 minutes until it starts to brown.
2. Add the onion, green pepper, ginger, and garlic and cook for 2 minutes.
3. In a small bowl, whisk together the tomato paste, rice vinegar, honey, and soy sauce.
4. Pour the mixture into the skillet and simmer for 5 minutes until it starts to thicken.
5. In a small bowl, whisk together the cornstarch and water.
6. Pour the mixture into the skillet and stir to combine. Simmer for 2 minutes until the stir fry has thickened.
7. Serve the stir fry with the chopped peanuts.

Nutrition information: (per serving) Calories: 229 kcal, Carbohydrates: 23.8 g, Protein: 15 g, Fat: 10 g, Saturated Fat: 1.3 g, Sodium: 587 mg, Potassium: 427 mg, Fiber: 4.5 g, Sugar: 7.7 g, Vitamin A: 305 IU, Vitamin C: 41.9 mg, Calcium: 124 mg, Iron: 2.5 mg

11. Jackfruit Carnitas Tacos

Jackfruit Carnitas Tacos are a delicious and easy vegan meal that is made with soft tacos, jackfruit, and a variety of spices for a flavorful and satisfying Mexican-inspired dish.
Serving: Serves 8
Preparation time: 10 mins
Ready time: 40 mins

Ingredients:
- 2 tablespoons olive oil
- 1 onion, diced
- 2 cloves garlic, minced
- 1 teaspoon ground cumin
- 1/2 teaspoon chili powder
- 1/4 teaspoon sea salt
- 1 (20-ounce) can jackfruit, drained and shredded
- 1/4 cup vegetable broth
- 1/2 cup jarred salsa
- 8 corn or flour soft taco shells
- 1/3 cup chopped fresh cilantro
- 1/2 cup diced red onion
- 1/2 cup diced avocado
- 1/4 cup crumbled cotija cheese

Instructions:
1. Heat the olive oil in a large skillet over medium heat. Add the onion and garlic and cook until softened, about 5 minutes.
2. Add the cumin, chili powder, and salt and cook for another minute.
3. Add the jackfruit and vegetable broth and cook for 10 minutes.
4. Add the salsa and cook for 5 minutes more.
5. Fill each taco shell with the jackfruit mixture and top with cilantro, red onion, avocado, and cotija cheese.

Nutrition information: Per serving: 231 calories, 11.9g fat, 28.8g carbohydrates, 5.5g protein, 5.3g fiber, 614mg sodium

12. Tempeh Bacon Breakfast Burrito

Start your day off right with this delicious Tempeh Bacon Breakfast Burrito that is filled with plant-based protein and smoky flavor.
Serving: Makes 1 burrito
Preparation Time: 10 minutes
Ready Time: 10 minutes

Ingredients:
- 2 Tbsp olive oil
- 2/3 cup tempeh bacon
- 1/3 cup cooked breakfast potatoes
- 2 eggs
- 1/4 tsp garlic powder
- 1/4 tsp onion powder
- 1/4 tsp smoked paprika
- A pinch of salt
- 1 medium-sized tortilla wrap
- 2 tbsp salsa
- 2 tbsp shredded cheese

Instructions:
1. In a small bowl, mix together garlic powder, onion powder, smoked paprika, and salt.
2. Heat the olive oil in a large skillet over medium-high heat. Add in the tempeh bacon and season with the spice mixture. Cook for 8 minutes, stirring occasionally, until crisp and slightly browned.
3. Reduce heat to medium-low and add in the cooked breakfast potatoes. Cook for 3 minutes, stirring occasionally, until potatoes are browned.
4. Push the tempeh bacon and potatoes to one side of the skillet. Crack two eggs into the skillet and season with the spice mixture. Scramble the eggs until cooked through.
5. Heat a tortilla wrap in microwave for 15-20 seconds until warm. Place the wrap onto a plate.
6. Add in the tempeh bacon and potatoes, followed by the scrambled eggs, salsa, and shredded cheese. Fold the wrap and enjoy!

Nutrition information: Calories- 550, Fat- 34 g, Protein- 29 g, Carbs-31 g, Sodium- 975 mg.

13. BBQ "Chick'n" Salad

Enjoy this savoury and delicious BBQ Chick'n Salad for a flavourful dinner! This dish is full of crunchy vegetables, sweet and spicy BBQ sauce, and succulent grilled chick'n.
Serving: Serves 4
Preparation Time: 10 minutes
Ready Time: 20 minutes

Ingredients:
- 2 large grilled chick'n breasts, sliced
- 2 cups romaine lettuce, chopped
- 1 cup corn kernels
- 1 cup red bell pepper, diced
- 1/2 cup cherry tomatoes, cut in half
- 1/4 cup red onion, diced
- 1/4 cup BBQ sauce

Instructions:
1. Grill two chicken breasts.
2. In a large bowl, combine lettuce, corn, bell pepper, tomatoes and red onion.
3. Slice the grilled chicken into thin strips.
4. Add the chicken, BBQ sauce and any additional desired seasoning into the bowl and mix well.
5. Serve chilled, topped with croutons if desired.

Nutrition information:
- Calories: 219 kcal
- Carbohydrates: 16 g
- Protein: 25 g
- Fat: 6 g
- Fiber: 4 g

14. Vegan "Beef" and Broccoli Stir Fry

This vegan "beef" and broccoli stir fry is a great vegan alternative to the classic beef and broccoli. This vegan dish is both delicious and filling, and is sure to please even the pickiest eaters.
Serving: Serves 4
Preparation time: 10 minutes
Ready time: 15 minutes

Ingredients:
- 1 package vegan "beef" strips
- 2 tablespoons vegetable oil
- 2 heads of broccoli, cut into florets
- 1/4 cup vegan oyster sauce
- 1 tablespoon soy sauce
- 1 teaspoon garlic powder
- 1 teaspoon ground ginger
- Salt and pepper, to taste

Instructions:
1. Heat oil in a large skillet over medium-high heat.
2. Add the vegan "beef" strips and cook until lightly browned, about 5 minutes.
3. Add the broccoli florets and cook until bright green and tender, about 5 minutes.
4. Add the oyster sauce, soy sauce, garlic powder, ginger, and salt and pepper and stir to combine.
5. Cook an additional 3-5 minutes, stirring occasionally.
6. Serve hot.

Nutrition information: Per serving: 250 calories, 11g fat, 4g saturated fat, 20g carbohydrate, 7g fiber, 5g sugar, 16g protein

15. Chickpea Tuna Salad Sandwich

This Chickpea Tuna Salad Sandwich is a delicious combination of chickpeas, tuna, and veggies topped with a creamy yogurt-based dressing and piled onto bread. It's a healthy, protein-packed meal that can be enjoyed any time of day!
Serving: 2

Preparation Time: 15 minutes
Ready Time: 15 minutes

Ingredients:
- 1 can (165 g) Chickpeas, rinsed and drained
- 1 can (185 g) solid light Tuna, drained
- ½ cup (120 ml) Plain Greek Yogurt
- 2 tbsp Mayonnaise
- 1 Celery Stalk, finely diced
- 1 Carrot, peeled and finely chopped
- 2 tbsp Green Onions, finely chopped
- 2 tsp Dijon Mustard
- 2 tsp Lemon Juice
- Salt and Pepper to taste
- 4 Sandwich Thins

Instructions:
1. In a medium bowl, mash the chickpeas with a fork.
2. Add in the tuna and stir until combined.
3. In a separate bowl, mix together the yogurt, mayonnaise, celery, carrot, green onions, mustard, lemon juice, salt, and pepper.
4. Add the dressing to the tuna and chickpea mixture and stir until combined.
5. Spread the mixture evenly between 2 sandwich thins, and serve.

Nutrition information (per serving):
Calories: 476
Total Fat: 20.3g
Carbohydrates: 39.8g
Protein: 39.2g
Sugar: 5.1g
Fiber: 10.9g
Cholesterol: 48.2mg

16. Vegan Sausage and Peppers

This vegan sausage and peppers dish is a delicious and vegan-friendly way to satisfy those Italian flavors! It's a great balanced meal with both protein and vegetables, and it's so simple to make.
Serving: 4-6
Preparation Time: 15 minutes
Ready Time: 15 minutes

Ingredients:
- 8 vegan sausages
- 4 bell peppers, sliced
- 2 onions, sliced
- 2 cloves of garlic, minced
- 2 tablespoons of olive oil
- Italian seasoning
- Salt and pepper, to taste

Instructions:
1. In a large skillet, heat the olive oil over medium heat.
2. Add the onions and peppers to the pan and cook for 5-7 minutes, stirring occasionally, until the vegetables begin to soften.
3. Add the garlic, Italian seasoning, salt, and pepper and continue to cook for 3-4 minutes, stirring occasionally.
4. Add the vegan sausages to the pan and cook for an additional 5-7 minutes, stirring occasionally, until the vegetables are fully cooked and the sausages are lightly browned.
5. Serve the vegan sausage and peppers with your favorite sides and enjoy!

Nutrition information:
Calories: 280 Kcal
Fat: 18 g
Carbohydrates: 13 g
Protein: 14 g
Fiber: 4 g
Sugar: 4 g

17. BBQ "Chick'n" Skewers

These BBQ "Chick'n" Skewers are the perfect dish to spice up an outdoor gathering. After marinating in a blend of flavorsome spices, tender pieces of seitan and vegetables are skewered and grilled to perfection for a flavorful and healthy meal.
Serving: 8 skewers
Preparation Time: 15 minutes
Ready Time: 30 minutes

Ingredients:
- 1 cup seitan, cut into cubes
- 2 bell peppers, stemmed, seeded, and cut into cubes
- 1 onion, cut into cubes
- 2 tablespoons olive oil
- 2 tablespoons soy sauce
- 1 tablespoon honey
- 1 tablespoon liquid smoke
- 2 teaspoons smoked paprika
- 1 tablespoon garlic powder

Instructions:
1. In a large bowl, combine the seitan, bell peppers, and onion.
2. In a separate bowl, whisk together the olive oil, soy sauce, honey, liquid smoke, smoked paprika, and garlic powder.
3. Pour the marinade over the seitan and vegetables and mix until everything is evenly coated.
4. Let the mixture marinate for 15 minutes.
5. Assemble the skewers, alternating seitan and vegetables.
6. Preheat the grill to medium-high heat.
7. Place the skewers on the grill and cook for 15-20 minutes, turning occasionally.

Nutrition information: Per skewer: 124 calories, 8.3g fat, 3.8 carbohydrates, 6.8 protein

18. Buffalo Chickpea Salad

Buffalo Chickpea Salad is a delicious and surprisingly easy to make salad that incorporates the zesty flavor of buffalo sauce with the savory

chickpeas. It's a crunchy, flavorful, and colorful dish that is sure to please any crowd.
Serving: 6-8
Preparation time: 10 minutes
Ready time: 30 minutes

Ingredients:
- 2 cans (15 oz.) chickpeas, drained and rinsed
- 1 cup cherry tomatoes, halved
- 1/2 cup ranch dressing
- 1/4 cup buffalo sauce
- 1/4 teaspoon black pepper
- 2 tablespoons diced red onion
- 2 tablespoons fresh parsley, chopped
- 1/4 cup crumbled feta cheese

Instructions:
1. Preheat oven to 375°F.
2. Spread chickpeas on a baking sheet.
3. Bake in the oven for 15 minutes.
4. Remove chickpeas from oven and let cool, about 10 minutes.
5. In a large bowl, combine ranch dressing, buffalo sauce, and black pepper until well incorporated.
6. Add chickpeas, tomatoes, red onion, parsley, and feta cheese and toss to coat.
7. Transfer salad to serving bowls and serve.

Nutrition information: 119 calories, 7.3g fat, 8.7g carbohydrates, 4.1g protein

19. Mushroom and Spinach Stuffed Shells

This Mushroom and Spinach Stuffed Shells recipe is a simple yet delicious dinner idea, with tender shells filled with a tasty and savory mixture of mushrooms, spinach, and cheeses. Perfect for weeknights or special occasions!
Serving: 4
Preparation time: 15 minutes

Ready time: 40 minutes

Ingredients:
- 12 jumbo or large shells
- 2 tablespoons olive oil
- 2 cloves garlic, minced
- 8 ounces crimini mushrooms, diced
- 2 cups baby spinach, chopped
- 1/2 cup mozzarella cheese, shredded
- 1/2 cup ricotta cheese
- 1/3 cup Parmesan cheese, shredded
- 2 teaspoons Italian herbs
- 1/4 teaspoon salt
- 2 tablespoons fresh parsley, chopped

Instructions:
1. Preheat the oven to 375F.
2. Cook the shells according to package instructions. Drain and rinse.
3. Heat the olive oil in a large skillet over medium-high heat. Add the garlic and mushrooms and cook for 5 minutes.
4. Add the spinach to the skillet and cook for an additional 2 minutes.
5. In a medium bowl, mix together the mozzarella, ricotta, Parmesan, herbs, and salt.
6. Fill each shell with the cheese mixture and place in a 9x13 inch baking dish.
7. Top with the mushroom and spinach mixture and sprinkle with parsley.
8. Bake for 25 minutes, or until the cheese is golden and bubbly.

Nutrition information:
Calories: 302, Fat: 12.3g, Saturated fat: 5.8g, Carbohydrates: 26.7g, Protein: 14.7g, Sodium: 343mg, Fiber: 1.8g.

20. Teriyaki Tofu Stir Fry

This delicious Teriyaki Tofu Stir Fry is a quick and easy to prepare dish that is packed with flavor. It is a great vegan and vegetarian alternative to your favorite Asian stir fry recipes.

Serving: 2
Preparation Time: 10 minutes
Ready Time: 15 minutes

Ingredients:
- 1 block of extra firm tofu (drained and pressed)*
- 2 tablespoons of vegetable or olive oil
- 2 cloves of garlic (minced)
- 2 tablespoons of teriyaki sauce
- 1 teaspoon of sesame oil
- 1/4 teaspoon of red pepper flakes
- 2 cups of vegetables (such as bell peppers, mushrooms, onions, and carrots)
- 1/4 cup of water
- 2 tablespoons of sesame seeds
- Salt and pepper to taste

Instructions:
1. Heat the oil in a large skillet over medium-high heat.
2. Add the garlic and red pepper flakes. Sauté until fragrant, about 1 minute.
3. Slice the tofu into cubes and add to the pan. Sauté until golden brown, about 5 minutes.
4. Add the teriyaki sauce, sesame oil, and vegetables. Sauté until the vegetables are tender, about 5 minutes.
5. Add the water and season with salt and pepper. Simmer for a few minutes until the liquid is reduced.
6. Remove from the heat and stir in the sesame seeds. Serve.

Nutrition information:
Calories: 196 kcal
Fat: 11.9 g
Carbohydrates: 12.3 g
Fiber: 5.6 g
Protein: 11.2 g

21. Vegan "Chicken" Parmesan

This delicious vegan version of the classic Chicken Parmesan recipe is made with vegan "chicken" patties that are breaded and then topped with marinara sauce and vegan mozzarella cheese.

Serving: 4
Preparation time: 15 minutes
Ready time: 25 minutes

Ingredients:
- 4 vegan "chicken" patties
- 2 cups dry breadcrumbs
- 1 tablespoon Italian seasoning
- 2 teaspoons garlic powder
- 2 tablespoons olive oil
- 2 cups marinara sauce
- 1 ½ cups vegan mozzarella

Instructions:
1. Preheat oven to 350°F (176°C).
2. Place the breadcrumbs in a shallow dish. Stir in Italian seasoning and garlic powder.
3. Heat the olive oil in a large skillet over medium heat.
4. Dip each vegan "chicken" patty into the breadcrumb mixture and press gently to coat. Place in skillet and cook until golden brown on both sides.
5. Place the vegan "chicken" patties in an oven-safe baking dish. Top with marinara sauce and vegan mozzarella.
6. Bake for 10 minutes, or until cheese is melted and bubbly.

Nutrition information: (per serving)
- Calories: 337 kcal
- Carbohydrates: 36.3 g
- Protein: 19.4 g
- Fat: 14.2 g
- Saturated Fat: 2.6 g
- Fiber: 3.4 g
- Sugar: 4.5 g
- Sodium: 982 mg

22. Spicy Sriracha Tofu

Spicy Sriracha Tofu is a delicious vegetarian dish that combines the sweet and hot flavors of Sriracha with the earthy taste of firm tofu. It's an easy meal to prepare with minimal Ingredients and no complicated cooking techniques.
Serving: 4
Preparation Time: 10 minutes
Ready Time: 20 minutes

Ingredients:
- 1 (14-ounce) block of extra-firm tofu
- 1/4 cup Sriracha
- 2 tablespoons olive oil
- 2 tablespoons lime juice
- 2 tablespoons honey
- 1 teaspoon salt

Instructions:
1. Preheat the oven to 400 degrees F. Line a baking sheet with parchment or foil.
2. Drain and press the tofu for 10 minutes. Cut it into 1-inch cubes.
3. In a small bowl, whisk together the Sriracha, olive oil, lime juice, honey, and salt.
4. Transfer the tofu to the baking sheet and drizzle the Sriracha mixture over the cubes.
5. Bake for 20 minutes, flipping the cubes halfway through.

Nutrition information: 252 kcal, 15 g fat, 19 g protein, 9 g carbohydrates, 0 g sugar.

23. Vegan "Meatball" Sub

This vegan "meatball" sub is the perfect mix of chewy, succulent vegan meatballs in a rich, tomato-y sauce, all topped off with melted vegan cheese! A hearty sandwich that will satisfy even the most hardcore carnivore.
Serving: Serves 4

Preparation time: 15 minutes
Ready time: 45 minutes

Ingredients:
- 1 package vegan meatballs
- 1/4 cup vegan Worcestershire sauce
- 1/4 cup tomato paste
- 1/4 cup diced tomatoes
- 1/4 cup vegan Parmesan cheese
- 1 teaspoon Italian seasoning
- 4 whole-wheat buns
- 1/4 cup vegan cheese, grated

Instructions:
1. Preheat oven to 375°F.
2. Arrange vegan meatballs on baking sheet and bake for 25 minutes, flipping once halfway through.
3. In a bowl, mix together Worcestershire sauce, tomato paste, diced tomatoes, vegan Parmesan cheese, and Italian seasoning.
4. Once vegan meatballs are done, add to the tomato mixture and stir until evenly coated.
5. Place each bun open-face on a baking sheet. Top each with a scoop of the vegan meatball mixture, followed by grated vegan cheese.
6. Bake for 10 minutes, or until cheese is melted.
7. Serve each open-face sub with additional toppings, if desired.

Nutrition information: Not available.

24. BBQ Cauliflower Bites

Get your barbecue on with these delicious BBQ Cauliflower Bites! Healthy, salty, and perfectly smoky, this fusion recipe is a must-try.
Serving: 4-6 people
Preparation Time: 10 minutes
Ready Time: 25 minutes

Ingredients:
- 1 large cauliflower head, cut into florets

- 3/4 cup breadcrumbs
- 1/4 cup plain flour
- 2 tablespoons vegetable oil
- 3/4 cup barbeque sauce
- 2 tablespoons melted butter
- 2 teaspoons smoked paprika
- 1 teaspoon garlic powder
- 1/4 teaspoon onion powder
- Salt and pepper to taste

Instructions:
1. Preheat the oven to 375°F (190°C). Line a baking tray with parchment paper and set aside.
2. In one bowl, mix together the breadcrumbs, flour, oil, mustard powder, smoked paprika, garlic powder, onion powder, salt, and pepper.
3. In another bowl, mix together the barbeque sauce and melted butter until well combined.
4. Take the cauliflower florets and dip them in the barbeque sauce mixture until each floret is well coated.
5. Transfer the coated florets to the prepared baking tray.
6. Sprinkle the breadcrumbs mixture over the florets.
7. Bake the florets in the preheated oven for 25 minutes, until golden brown and crispy.

Nutrition information: per serving – 157 calories, 7.2g fat, 17.8g carbohydrates, 3.3g protein

25. Seitan Philly Cheesesteak

Traditional Philly cheesesteak has been given a vegan twist with this delicious seitan version. Packed with protein and flavour, it will make your taste buds sing!
Serving: 6
Preparation time: 5 minutes
Ready time: 20 minutes

Ingredients:
- 2 tbsp olive oil

- 500g seitan mince
- 1 onion, finely diced
- 2 cloves garlic, minced
- 120ml vegetable stock
- 2 tbsp vegan Worcestershire sauce
- 1 tbsp soy sauce
- 1 green capsicum, diced
- 6 vegan cheese slices
- 6 vegan burger buns

Instructions:
1. Heat the oil in a large skillet over medium heat and add the seitan mince, onion and garlic. Cook for 5 minutes, stirring often.
2. Pour the vegetable stock, Worcestershire sauce and soy sauce into the pan and stir.
3. Add the capsicum and cook for another 5 minutes.
4. Place vegan cheese slices onto the buns and spoon the seitan mixture onto it.
5. Place the buns onto a baking tray and cook for 5-10 minutes, or until the cheese is melted and bubbling.

Nutrition information (per serving):
- Calories: 340 kcal
- Fat: 16 g
- Carbohydrates: 27 g
- Fiber: 1.9 g
- Protein: 28.3 g

26. Coconut Curry Chickpea Stew

This flavorful Coconut Curry Chickpea Stew is a deliciously savory and creamy stew that can be served with warm naan or basmati rice. It's packed with nutrient-dense Ingredients and spices that make it a healthy vegan meal perfect for any night of the week.
Serving: 4-6
Preparation Time: 10 mins
Ready Time: 30 mins

Ingredients:
- 1 tablespoon olive oil
- 1 onion, diced
- 2 cloves garlic, minced
- 1 teaspoon fresh ginger, grated
- 2 teaspoons curry powder
- 1 teaspoon garam masala
- 1/2 teaspoon ground cumin
- 1 teaspoon turmeric powder
- 2 red bell peppers, diced
- 2 cans of chickpeas, drained & rinsed
- 1 can coconut milk
- 2 cups vegetable stock
- 1 lime, juiced
- Salt, to taste
- Fresh cilantro, for garnish

Instructions:
1. Heat the olive oil in a large pot over medium-high heat. Once hot, add the onion and sauté for 3-4 minutes until softened.
2. Add the garlic and ginger, and cook for an additional minute.
3. Add the curry powder, garam masala, cumin, and turmeric and stir until everything is well combined.
4. Add the bell pepper, chickpeas, coconut milk, and vegetable stock. Stir everything together and allow the stew to come to a bubble.
5. Reduce the heat to low and simmer, covered, for 25 minutes.
6. Once cooked, stir in the lime juice and add salt, to taste.
7. Serve over warm basmati rice or with some warm naan, and top with fresh cilantro for garnish.

Nutrition information:
- Calories: 200
- Total Fat: 11.2g
- Saturated Fat: 8.3g
- Sodium: 608mg
- Potassium: 354mg
- Carbohydrates: 22.2g
- Fiber: 3.8g
- Sugar: 4.8g
- Protein: 4.3g

27. Vegan Breakfast Sausage Patties

Start your day off right with these delicious and easy to make vegan breakfast sausage patties! They are made with simple pantry staples, and are packed full of protein and flavor! Servings: 8-10 patties Preparation Time: 10 minutes Ready Time: 35 minutes

Ingredients:
- 1 tablespoon olive oil
- 1/2 cup diced yellow onion
- 2 cloves garlic, minced
- 1/4 teaspoon dried thyme
- 1 teaspoon smoked paprika
- 1/4 teaspoon ground nutmeg
- 1/4 teaspoon black pepper
- 2 cups cooked rice
- 1 cup cooked mashed sweet potatoes
- 1/2 cup vegan sausage crumbles (We recommend Beyond sausage crumbles)
- 1/4 teaspoon sea salt
- 2 tablespoons ground flaxseed

Instructions:
1. Heat the oil in a large skillet over medium heat. Add the onion and sauté until softened.
2. Add the garlic, thyme, paprika, nutmeg, and pepper. Sauté for another two minutes, stirring frequently.
3. Add the cooked rice, mashed sweet potatoes, vegan sausage crumbles, sea salt, and ground flaxseed to the skillet. Mix together until everything is well incorporated.
4. Use a spoon or large cookie scoop to scoop the mixture into the skillet, forming round patties.
5. Cook on each side for 5-7 minutes until golden brown and heated through.
6. Serve warm with your favorite side dishes.

Nutrition information: per serving (1 patty): 120 calories, 5g fat, 16g carbohydrates, 2g fiber, 5g protein.

28. Vegan "Beef" Fajitas

Spice up your meat-free meal plan with this delicious vegan "beef" fajita recipe! Crafted with soy-based vegan "beef" crumble, veggies, and flavorful spices, these fajitas make a great easy, healthy dinner for two.
Serving: 2
Preparation Time: 20 minutes
Ready Time: 20 minutes

Ingredients:
- 1 package vegan "beef" crumbles
- 4 whole wheat or corn tortillas
- 1 red bell pepper, julienned
- 1 yellow onion, chopped
- 1 tablespoon olive oil
- 1 teaspoon ground cumin
- ½ teaspoon chili powder
- ½ teaspoon garlic powder
- Salt and pepper, to taste
- ½ lime, juiced
- Optional: ¼ cup cilantro, chopped

Instructions:
1. Heat a large skillet over medium-high heat and add in vegan beef crumbles. Cook for 5 minutes or until lightly browned.
2. Remove beef from the pan and set aside.
3. Add oil, bell pepper, onion, cumin, chili powder, garlic powder, a pinch of salt, and pepper to the skillet. Cook for 5 minutes, stirring occasionally.
4. Return vegan "beef" crumbles to the skillet and mix everything together.
5. Remove pan from heat and stir in lime juice.
6. Serve vegan "beef" fajitas on warm tortillas and top with cilantro.

Nutrition information:

Calories: 330, Carbs: 39g, Protein: 22g, Fat: 14g, Sodium: 42mg, Fiber: 10g

29. Smoky Chipotle Tempeh Tacos

These Smoky Chipotle Tempeh Tacos are the perfect plant-based meal for any time of day. Full of flavor and packed with plant-based proteins, these tacos will hit the spot!
Serving: 4
Preparation time: 10 minutes
Ready time: 20 minutes

Ingredients:
- 8-10 small corn tortillas
- 8 ounces tempeh, crumbled
- 2 tablespoons of olive oil
- 2 teaspoons of smoked paprika
- 1 teaspoon of ground chipotle
- 1 teaspoon of garlic powder
- 1 teaspoon of onion powder
- 2 tablespoons of tamari or soy sauce
- 1/2 cup of tomato or salsa

Instructions:
1. Preheat the oven to 350°F.
2. In a bowl, mix the crumbled tempeh with the smoked paprika, ground chipotle, garlic powder, onion powder, and tamari or soy sauce.
3. Heat the olive oil in a pan over medium heat.
4. Add the tempeh mixture to the pan and cook for 8-10 minutes, stirring occasionally.
5. Place the corn tortillas onto a baking sheet and bake for 5 minutes.
6. Take the corn tortillas out of the oven and place the cooked tempeh onto the tortillas.
7. Serve the tacos with salsa or tomato sauce and your favorite toppings.

Nutrition information: Serving size - 2 tacos: Calories 243, Total Fat 12 g, Saturated Fat 2 g, Cholesterol 0 mg, Sodium 407 mg,

Total Carbohydrate 23 g, Dietary Fiber 4 g, Sugars 3 g, Protein 11 g.

30. Jackfruit Crab Cakes

Jackfruit Crab Cakes are an amazing fusion between two regional favorites. These patties are crisp on the outside with a soft interior. The jackfruit adds a subtle sweetness that makes them unique & delicious.
Serving: Makes 2 medium Crab Cakes
Preparation Time: 10 minutes
Ready Time: 25 minutes

Ingredients:
- 1 ½ cups canned jackfruit
- ½ cup red onion, diced
- 2 garlic cloves, minced
- 1 cup cooked baby spinach
- 2 tablespoons Dijon mustard
- 2 tablespoons mayonnaise
- ½ teaspoon each of paprika, garlic powder & onion powder
- 1 tablespoon fresh dill, chopped
- 1 tablespoon fresh parsley, chopped
- ½ cup panko crumbs
- 2 tablespoons vegan parmesan cheese
- 2 tablespoons olive oil

Instructions:
1. Preheat oven to 375°F.
2. In a medium bowl, combine jackfruit, onion, garlic, spinach, mustard, mayonnaise, seasonings, and herbs.
3. Mix until all Ingredients are combined and season to taste with salt & pepper.
4. In a separate bowl, mix together the panko crumbs and vegan parmesan cheese.
5. Divide the jackfruit mixture into two equal portions and form each into a patty.
6. Coat each patty with panko-parm mixture and place on a greased baking sheet.

7. Brush the tops with olive oil and bake for 20 minutes.
8. Let cool for 5 minutes before serving.

Nutrition information:
- Calories: 298
- Fat: 13g
- Carbohydrates: 36g
- Protein: 7g

31. Tempeh Bacon BLT Sandwich

This delicious Tempeh Bacon BLT Sandwich is a great twist on the classic sandwich. It's vegan, gluten free, and full of protein-rich and flavorful tempeh!
Serving: 2
Preparation time: 10 minutes
Ready time: 10 minutes

Ingredients:
- 2 slices tempeh bacon
- 1/2 avocado, sliced
- 1/4 cup vegan mayonnaise
- 2 slices of tomato
- 2 lettuce leaves
- 2 slices of bread

Instructions:
1. Heat a large skillet over medium heat.
2. Add the tempeh bacon slices and cook for about 5 minutes, or until crispy. Flip and cook for an additional 5 minutes.
3. Meanwhile, spread mayonnaise on one side of each slice of bread.
4. Assemble the sandwich by layering the lettuce, tomato, avocado, and tempeh bacon on one slice of bread.
5. Top with the other slice of bread and press lightly. Cut in half and serve.

Nutrition information: Each sandwich contains 397 calories, 21g fat, 10g protein, and 41g carbohydrates.

32. Vegan "Chicken" Enchiladas

Let's get a taste of traditional Mexican cuisine with this delicious vegan enchiladas. Tastefully stuffed with vegan "chicken" and cheese, it's the perfect dish for a health-conscious meal.

Serving: 4
Preparation Time: 10 minutes
Ready Time: 25 minutes

Ingredients:
- 2 tablespoons olive oil
- 2 cloves garlic, minced
- 2 cups vegan "chicken"
- 2 tablespoons taco seasoning
- 1/4 teaspoon chili powder
- 1/4 teaspoon cumin
- 12 6-inch corn tortillas
- 2 cups vegan cheese
- 1 15-ounce can enchilada sauce
- 1/4 cup chopped fresh cilantro (optional)

Instructions:
1. Preheat oven to 350°F.
2. Heat olive oil in a large skillet over medium heat.
3. Add the garlic and cook for 1 minute.
4. Add the vegan "chicken" and season with taco seasoning, chili powder and cumin.
5. Cook for 5 minutes, stirring occasionally.
6. Take off heat and set aside.
7. Place a tortilla in a greased baking dish, top with cooked vegan "chicken", sprinkle with cheese and pour a spoon of enchilada sauce over the top.
8. Repeat with the remaining tortillas.
9. Bake for 25 minutes, until edges begin to brown.
10. Drizzle with additional enchilada sauce and cilantro (optional).

Nutrition information:

Calories: 406, Fat: 25.3g, Protein: 14.2g, Carbohydrate: 28.4g, Sugar: 3.6g, Sodium: 840mg, Fiber: 5.4g

33. Korean BBQ Tofu Lettuce Wraps

Enjoy this delicious and healthy Korean BBQ tofu lettuce wraps. It's savory, sweet, and has the perfect crunch. A perfect summer meal or dinner when you want something light and healthy. Servings: 8 Preparation Time: 10 minutes Ready Time: 25 minutes

Ingredients:
- 2 tablespoons vegetable oil
- 1 package of extra-firm tofu (about 14 ounces), drained and cut into cubes
- 2 cloves garlic, finely chopped
- 1 tablespoon fresh ginger, finely chopped
- 1/4 cup soy sauce
- 2 tablespoons honey
- 1 teaspoon sesame oil
- 1 teaspoon rice vinegar
- 2 tablespoons sesame seeds
- 1 teaspoon chili pepper flakes
- 8 lettuce leaves

Instructions:
1. In a medium skillet, heat the vegetable oil over medium-high heat.
2. Add the tofu cubes and cook until lightly browned, about 5 minutes.
3. Add the garlic and ginger and cook for another minute.
4. Add the soy sauce, honey, sesame oil, and rice vinegar and stir to combine.
5. Cook the mixture for 3 minutes, stirring occasionally.
6. Remove from the heat and stir in the sesame seeds and chili pepper flakes.
7. To serve, spoon the tofu mixture into the lettuce leaves.

Nutrition information: Per serving, 154.5 calories, 8.9 g fat, 14.4 g carbohydrates, 8.2 g protein, 2.5 g fiber.

34. BBQ "Chick'n" Pizza

This delicious BBQ Chick'n Pizza is perfect for any pizza night. It's loaded with bbq sauced chicken, creamy cheese, and all the veggies you could ask for.
Serving: Serves 8
Preparation time: 20 minutes
Ready time: 35 minutes

Ingredients:
- 1 pound boneless, skinless chicken breasts
- 1/2 cup BBQ sauce
- 2 cups shredded mozzarella cheese
- 1/2 cup thinly sliced bell peppers
- 1/4 cup sliced red onion
- 1/4 cup quartered cherry tomatoes
- 1/4 cup chopped fresh parsley
- 1 teaspoon garlic powder
- 1 (14-inch) pre-made pizza crust
- 1 tablespoon olive oil

Instructions:
1. Preheat the oven to 425°F, and lightly grease a baking sheet.
2. Arrange the chicken breasts on the baking sheet and brush with bbq sauce. Next, sprinkle on garlic powder and bake for 15-20 minutes until the chicken is cooked through.
3. Once the chicken is cooked, remove from the oven and cut into small cubes then set aside.
4. Place the pizza crust onto the baking sheet and brush with olive oil. Top the pizza with the diced chicken, mozzarella cheese, bell peppers, red onion, and tomatoes.
5. Bake for 14-16 minutes until the cheese is melty and golden. Top with chopped parsley and serve hot.

Nutrition information:
Calories: 390, Fat: 9g, Saturated Fat: 4g, Carbohydrates: 41g, Protein: 28g, Cholesterol: 64mg, Sodium: 799mg, Fiber: 2g, Sugar: 11g.

35. Vegan Sloppy Joes

Enjoy the classic flavor of Sloppy Joes made vegan with these delicious vegan Sloppy Joes. Easy to make and sure to be a hit with everyone, these vegan Sloppy Joes are a great way to please everyone.
Serving: Makes 4 Sandwich portions
Preparation Time: 10 minutes
Ready Time: 20 minutes

Ingredients:
- 1 tablespoon olive oil
- 1 onion, finely diced
- 2 cloves garlic, minced
- 1 red bell pepper, chopped
- 1 green bell pepper, chopped
- 1/2 teaspoon smoked paprika
- 1/2 teaspoon chili powder
- 1 (15 oz) can of lentils, drained and rinsed
- 1 (15 oz) can tomato sauce
- 2 tablespoons tomato paste
- 2 tablespoons vegan Worcestershire sauce
- ¼ cup packed dark brown sugar
- 2 teaspoons yellow mustard
- Salt and pepper, to taste
- 4 vegan slider buns

Instructions:
1. Heat the olive oil in a large skillet over medium heat. Add the onion and garlic and cook until they are soft and fragrant, about 5 minutes.
2. Add the bell peppers, paprika, and chili powder and cook for an additional 5 minutes.
3. Add the lentils, tomato sauce, tomato paste, vegan Worcestershire sauce, brown sugar, and mustard. Simmer the mixture on low heat for 10 minutes or until the lentils are tender and the sauce is thick.
4. Season the mixture with salt and pepper, to taste.
5. Serve the mixture on vegan slider buns.

Nutrition information: Contains: 188 calories, 6g fat, 31g carbohydrates, 7g protein, and 8g fiber.

36. Chickpea and Vegetable Curry

Chickpea and Vegetable Curry is a classic Indian vegan dish that can be cooked on the stovetop or in a slow cooker. It is full of flavor, nutritious, and satisfying.
Serving: Serves 6-8
Preparation time: 10 minutes
Ready time: 45 minutes

Ingredients:
- 2 tablespoons olive oil
- 1 medium onion, diced
- 3 cloves garlic, minced
- 1 teaspoon ginger, minced
- 2 tablespoons curry powder
- 1 teaspoon smoked paprika
- 1 teaspoon garam masala
- 1/2 teaspoon turmeric
- 1/2 teaspoon chili powder
- 1/2 teaspoon sea salt
- 4 cups of mixed vegetables, chopped (e.g. bell peppers, carrots, cauliflower, zucchini, snow peas, etc.)
- 1 (14-ounce) can diced tomatoes
- 2 (14-ounce) cans chickpeas, rinsed and drained
- 2 cups vegetable broth
- 2 tablespoons freshly squeezed lemon juice
- Chopped fresh cilantro, for serving

Instructions:
1. Heat olive oil in a large pot over medium heat. Add onion and sauté for 3 minutes.
2. Add garlic, ginger, curry powder, smoked paprika, garam masala, turmeric, chili powder, and salt and cook for 1 more minute.
3. Add the vegetables and cook for 5 minutes.

4. Add the tomatoes, chickpeas, and vegetable broth, and bring to a boil. Reduce the heat to low and simmer for 30 minutes, until the vegetables are tender.
5. Turn off the heat and stir in the lemon juice. Serve over cooked grains or rice with chopped fresh cilantro, if desired.

Nutrition information:
- Calories per serving: 322
- Fat: 7 g
- Carbs: 45 g
- Fiber: 11 g
- Protein: 13 g

37. Vegan "Meatball" Spaghetti

Savory and hearty vegan "meatball" spaghetti is a delicious, meat-free alternative to the classic Italian dish. This vegan version still has all of the flavor and is just as filling and satisfying as the traditional dish.
Serving: Serves 6
Preparation Time: 10 minutes
Ready Time: 30 minutes

Ingredients:
-2 tablespoons of olive oil
-1 onion, diced
-2 cloves garlic, minced
-1 package of vegan ground "meat"
-1 can crushed tomatoes
-1 teaspoon dried oregano
-1 teaspoon dried basil
-¼ cup nutritional yeast
-salt and pepper to taste
-12 ounces spaghetti noodles

Instructions:
1. Heat the olive oil in a large skillet over medium-high heat.
2. Add the onion and garlic to the skillet and sauté for about 5 minutes, or until the onion is soft and translucent.

3. Add the vegan "meat" to the skillet and cook for a few minutes, stirring often, until the vegan "meat" is lightly browned.
4. Add the crushed tomatoes, oregano, basil, nutritional yeast, salt, and pepper to the skillet. Reduce heat to low and simmer for 15 minutes.
5. While the sauce is simmering, cook the spaghetti noodles according to the package directions.
6. Drain the noodles and add to the skillet with the sauce. Mix together until the noodles are evenly coated.
7. Serve the vegan "meatball" spaghetti with a sprinkle of extra nutritional yeast, if desired.

Nutrition information: 290 calories per serving, 16grams fat, 14grams of protein, 35grams of carbohydrates.

38. Buffalo Cauliflower Salad

Buffalo Cauliflower Salad is the perfect mix of spicy, crunchy, and creamy, and it's both vegan and gluten-free. Even better, it's both quick and easy to prepare.
Serving: Serves 4-6
Preparation time: 10 minutes
Ready time: 15 minutes

Ingredients:
- 1 head of cauliflower, broken up into florets
- 2 cloves garlic, minced
- 1/2 teaspoon chili powder
- 1/2 teaspoon paprika
- 1/4 teaspoon cayenne pepper
- 1/4 teaspoon thyme
- 1/4 teaspoon salt
- 1/4 cup olive oil
- 1/2 cup hot sauce
- 2 tablespoons apple cider vinegar
- 2 tablespoons vegan mayo
- 1/4 cup chopped green onion
- 1/4 cup chopped fresh parsley

Instructions:
1. Preheat oven to 425°F.
2. In a large bowl, combine cauliflower florets, minced garlic, chili powder, paprika, cayenne pepper, thyme, salt, and olive oil. Toss until cauliflower is evenly coated.
3. Place coated cauliflower on a greased baking sheet and bake for 15 minutes, flipping halfway through.
4. In a separate bowl, whisk together hot sauce, apple cider vinegar, vegan mayo, green onion, and parsley.
5. Once cauliflower is done baking, transfer to a large bowl and pour hot sauce mixture over it. Toss until cauliflower is evenly coated.
6. Serve hot or cold.

Nutrition information: Calories: 202, Fat: 14g, Carbohydrates: 13g, Protein: 4g, Sodium: 670mg, Fiber: 4g.

39. Teriyaki Tofu Noodle Bowl

This delicious teriyaki tofu noodle bowl is a fragrant combination of noodles, tofu, vegetables and a deliciously sweet glaze sauce.
Serving: 4
Preparation time: 10 minutes
Ready time: 20 minutes

Ingredients:
- 9 oz firm tofu, drained and pressed
- 3 teaspoons teriyaki sauce
- 2 tablespoons extra-virgin olive oil
- 1/2 red onion, diced
- 2 cloves garlic, minced
- 2 carrots, julienned
- 3 1/2 oz dried soba noodles
- 2 scallions, thinly sliced
- 2 tablespoons chopped sesame seeds

Instructions:
1. Preheat the oven to 375°F.

2. Cut the tofu into cubes. Place them on a baking sheet greased with olive oil. Drizzle with teriyaki sauce and bake for 20 minutes, turning once.
3. Heat olive oil in a saucepan. Add red onion and sauté for 3 minutes.
4. Add garlic, carrots and noodles. Sauté for 3 minutes more.
5. Pour in 2 cups of water and simmer for 10 minutes until the noodles are softened.
6. Add roasted tofu to the pan and stir in scallions. Simmer for another few minutes until everything is warmed through.
7. Serve the noodle bowl in individual bowls and garnish with sesame seeds.

Nutrition information: Calories: 259; Total Fat: 11g; Saturated Fat: 2g; Cholesterol: 0mg; Sodium: 328mg; Carbohydrates: 28g; Fiber: 4g; Sugar: 3g; Protein: 11g.

40. Vegan "Beef" Stir Fry

This vegan "beef" stir fry is a tasty and quick dish sure to please anyone looking for a delicious plant-based meal. It features an array of vegetables, vegan "beef" strips, and tasty Asian-inspired sauces that come together in less than 30 minutes!
Serving: 4-6
Preparation time: 10 minutes
Ready time: 20 minutes

Ingredients:
- 2 tablespoons sesame oil
- 1 package vegan "beef" strips
- 2 cloves garlic, minced
- 2 bell peppers, cut into strips
- 2 carrots, cut into matchsticks
- 2 cups mushrooms, sliced
- ½ cup vegan beef-style broth
- 2 tablespoons soy sauce
- 2 tablespoons agave or maple syrup
- 1 teaspoon chili flakes

Instructions:
1. Heat the sesame oil in a large skillet over medium heat.
2. Add the vegan "beef" strips and garlic, and cook for 3-4 minutes until the vegan "beef" is lightly browned.
3. Add the bell peppers, carrots, mushrooms and stir fry for 3-4 minutes.
4. Add the vegan beef-style broth, soy sauce, agave or maple syrup and chili flakes to the skillet and continue to stir fry for 2-3 more minutes until everything is cooked through.
5. Serve with your favorite sides and enjoy!

Nutrition information: This vegan "Beef" stir fry is packed with vitamins and minerals. It is a good source of vitamins A, C, B6, and fiber. It contains no cholesterol and is low in saturated fat.

41. Seitan Gyro Wrap

Seitan Gyro Wrap is a delicious middle-eastern inspired vegetarian dish that's packed with nutrition and flavor. It features a wheat-based seitan and is wrapped up in a warm pita with hummus, cucumbers, onions, and tomatoes.

Serving: Serves 2
Preparation Time: 10 minutes
Ready Time: 10 minutes

Ingredients:
- 2 8-inch wholewheat pita breads
- 4 ounces seitan, sliced
- 2 tablespoons hummus
- 1/4 cup cucumber, sliced
- 1/4 cup onion, sliced
- 1/4 cup tomatoes, sliced
- 2 teaspoons olive oil

Instructions:
1. Preheat a large skillet over medium-high heat.
2. Brush each pita bread with a teaspoon of olive oil. Place on hot skillet and cook for 2 minutes each side, then remove from heat.

3. Place seitan slices into the same skillet and cook for 2-3 minutes each side until golden.
4. To assemble the gyros, spread hummus on each pita bread and top with seitan, cucumber, onion, and tomato slices.
5. Wrap each pita tightly and serve.

Nutrition information: (per serving) Calories: 233; Fat: 5.4g; Carbohydrates: 34g; Protein: 12g

42. BBQ Jackfruit Sliders

BBQ Jackfruit Sliders are a tasty vegan alternative to meat-based sliders. It is a sweet and savory dish that is sure to please anyone on the lookout for a tasty snack.
Serving: 6
Preparation Time: 10 minutes
Ready Time: 20 minutes

Ingredients:
- 2 20-oz cans young jackfruit in water
- 2 tablespoons olive oil
- 1 teaspoon smoked paprika
- 1 teaspoon onion powder
- 1 teaspoon garlic powder
- 1 teaspoon chili powder
- 1/2 teaspoon sea salt
- 1/2 cup barbecue sauce plus 1/4 cup for basting
- 6 vegan slider buns

Instructions:
1. Preheat oven to 375°F.
2. Drain the canned jackfruit in a colander.
3. In a medium bowl, combine the olive oil, smoked paprika, onion powder, garlic powder, chili powder and sea salt.
4. Add the drained jackfruit and toss to evenly coat.
5. Place the jackfruit onto a parchment-lined baking sheet.
6. Bake in the preheated oven for 20 minutes, flipping the jackfruit once halfway through.

7. Remove pan from the oven and add 1/2 cup of barbecue sauce.
8. Toss the jackfruit in the sauce to evenly coat.
9. Place the jackfruit on slider buns and top with extra barbecue sauce for basting.

Nutrition information:
Calories: 350, Fat: 7g, Saturated Fat: 1g, Sodium: 600mg, Carbohydrates: 57g, Fiber: 6g, Sugar: 10g, Protein:6g

43. Spicy Buffalo Tofu Nuggets

Spicy Buffalo Tofu Nuggets are a vegan twist on a classic dish; they are packed with flavor and make a great appetizer or side dish.
Serving: 4
Preparation Time: 10 minutes
Ready Time: 25 minutes

Ingredients:
- 1 16-ounce package extra-firm tofu, frozen, thawed, and pressed
- 2 tablespoons vegetable oil
- 1/2 cup panko bread crumbs
- 1/4 cup all-purpose flour
- 1/4 teaspoon garlic powder
- 1/4 teaspoon smoked paprika
- 1/4 teaspoon cayenne pepper
- 1/2 teaspoon salt
- 1/2 cup hot sauce
- 2 tablespoons vegan butter, melted

Instructions:
1. Preheat the oven to 425°F. Line a baking sheet with parchment paper.
2. Cut the tofu into 1-inch cubes.
3. In a shallow bowl, mix together the panko bread crumbs, flour, garlic powder, smoked paprika, cayenne pepper, and salt.
4. In a separate bowl, mix together the hot sauce and melted vegan butter.
5. Dip each tofu cube into the hot sauce mixture, then roll it in the panko mixture, pressing to coat. Place on the prepared baking sheet.

6. Bake for 20 minutes, or until the coating is golden and crispy.
7. Serve hot and enjoy!

Nutrition information:
Calories: 390; Fat: 23g; Carbs: 29g; Protein: 17g

44. Vegan Breakfast Burrito Bowl

Enjoy a filling and healthy vegan breakfast with this easy and delicious burrito bowl. It's packed with nutritious Ingredients and flavorful seasonings for a hearty breakfast that will keep you full until lunch.
Serving: 4
Preparation Time: 15 minutes
Ready Time: 15 minutes

Ingredients:
- ¼ cup uncooked lentils
- 1 cup cooked quinoa
- 2 tablespoons olive oil
- ½ teaspoon ground cumin
- ½ teaspoon smoked paprika
- ½ teaspoon garlic powder
- ¼ teaspoon salt
- 1 red bell pepper, diced
- 1 15-ounce can black beans, drained and rinsed
- 1 cup cherry tomatoes, halved
- 1 avocado, diced
- 2 tablespoons fresh lime juice
- Handful fresh cilantro, roughly chopped

Instructions:
1. Place the lentils in a medium saucepan and cover with water. Bring to a boil and simmer until the lentils are tender, about 10 minutes. Drain any excess water.
2. Meanwhile, cook the quinoa according to package instructions.
3. In a large skillet, heat the olive oil over medium heat. Add the cooked lentils, cumin, smoked paprika, garlic powder, and salt. Cook for 2 minutes, stirring occasionally.

4. Add the bell pepper, black beans, and tomatoes to the skillet. Cook for 5 minutes, stirring occasionally.
5. To assemble the bowls, divide the quinoa among four bowls. Top with the lentil mixture, avocado, fresh lime juice, and cilantro.
6. Serve immediately.

Nutrition information (per serving): Calories 300, Total Fat 12g, Saturated Fat 2g, Cholesterol 0mg, Sodium 120mg, Total Carbohydrate 38g, Dietary Fiber 8g, Protein 9g.

45. Chickpea Shawarma Wrap

Chickpea Shawarma Wrap is a nutritious and delicious wrap recipe that showcases the unique Middle Eastern flavor. The main ingredients are chickpeas, hummus, and tahini, which give a healthy twist to a classic wrap.
Serving: 2
Preparation Time: 15 minutes
Ready Time: 25 minutes

Ingredients:
-1 can (15 ounces) chickpeas, drained
-3 tablespoons hummus
-1 tablespoon tahini
-1/4 teaspoon ground cumin
-1/4 teaspoon paprika
-1/2 avocado, sliced
-1/4 red onion, sliced
-2 tablespoons chopped parsley
-2 wrap/tortilla wraps

Instructions:
1. Preheat oven to 375 degrees F.
2. In a small bowl, combine the chickpeas, hummus, tahini, cumin, and paprika.
3. Spread the chickpea mixture evenly on the wrap/tortillas.
4. Top with avocado, red onion, and parsley.
5. Roll up wraps and place on a baking sheet.

6. Bake in preheated oven for 8-10 minutes until wraps are lightly toasted.
7. Slice wraps in half and serve.

Nutrition information:
Each serving contains: Calories: 280; Protein: 8 g; Total Fat: 12 g; Total Carbohydrates: 31 g; Fiber: 7 g; Sodium: 172 mg

46. Vegan "Chicken" Caesar Salad

Indulge in this vegan "chicken" Caesar salad that is quick and easy to make! This flavorful vegan-friendly salad is a healthier twist on the popular classic that will leave you feeling satisfied.
Serving: 4
Preparation time: 10 minutes
Ready time: 10 minutes

Ingredients:
- 2 cups vegan "chicken" strips
- 1 head romaine lettuce, washed & chopped
- 2 cloves garlic, minced
- 2 tablespoons olive oil
- 2 tablespoons vegan mayonnaise
- 2 tablespoons vegan Parmesan
- 1/4 teaspoon sea salt
- 1/4 teaspoon ground black pepper

Instructions:
1. Preheat the oven to 400° F (200° C). Place the vegan "chicken" strips on a baking sheet lined with parchment paper and bake for 10 minutes.
2. In a large bowl, combine the lettuce, garlic, olive oil, mayonnaise, vegan Parmesan, sea salt, and ground black pepper and toss to combine.
3. Add the baked vegan "chicken" strips to the bowl and toss to coat.
4. Divide the salad among four bowls, top with additional vegan Parmesan, and serve.

Nutrition information:

Calories: 160, Fat: 11g, Carbohydrates: 5g, Protein: 9g, Fiber: 2g, Sugar: 1g, Sodium: 144mg

47. Coconut Curry Lentil Soup

This delicious Coconut Curry Lentil Soup is a vegan & gluten-free soup that packs a flavorful punch. It's easy to make and is perfect for lunch or dinner to give you the nutrition and flavor you need.
Serving: 6
Preparation time: 10 minutes
Ready time: 40 minutes

Ingredients:
- 2 cups of green lentils
- 2 tablespoons of olive oil
- 1 small onion, diced
- 2 cloves of garlic, minced
- 1 tablespoon of ginger, grated
- 1 tablespoon of curry powder
- 2 teaspoons of sea salt
- 1 can of light coconut milk
- 2 cups of vegetable broth
- 2 tablespoons of tomato paste

Instructions:
1. In a medium saucepan, heat the olive oil over medium heat.
2. Add the onion and garlic, and sauté for 1-2 minutes until fragrant.
3. Add the ginger and curry powder, and stir to combine.
4. Add the green lentils, salt, coconut milk, and vegetable broth.
5. Raise the heat to high and bring to a boil.
6. Once the soup has come to a boil, reduce to a simmer, and simmer for 30 minutes, or until the lentils are soft.
7. Add the tomato paste and stir to combine.
8. Serve the soup hot, with your favorite toppings.

Nutrition information:
Per serving: 275 calories; 11.7 g fat; 34 g carbohydrates; 9.5 g protein

48. Vegan Sausage Breakfast Skillet

Enjoy a vegan-friendly breakfast with this easy-to-make vegan sausage breakfast skillet. This dish will become your go-to for a tasty morning meal.

Serving: 4
Preparation time: 10 minutes
Ready time: 30 minutes

Ingredients:
- 2 tablespoons olive oil
- 1 onion, diced
- 4 vegan sausages, sliced
- 2 cloves garlic, minced
- 4 medium potatoes, diced
- 1 teaspoon Italian seasoning
- 1/2 teaspoon paprika
- Salt and pepper, to taste
- 1/4 cup vegan cheese, optional

Instructions:
1. Preheat the oven to 375°F.
2. Heat the olive oil in a large skillet over medium-high heat.
3. Add the onion and vegan sausages, cooking for about 5 minutes.
4. Add in the garlic, potatoes, Italian seasoning, paprika, salt, and pepper. Toss to combine.
5. Cook for about 10 minutes, until potatoes are cooked through.
6. Top with vegan cheese, if desired.
7. Transfer to the preheated oven and bake for 15 minutes.

Nutrition information (per serving): Calories: 260, Fat: 15g, Saturated Fat: 2g, Carbohydrates: 21g, Fiber: 3g, Sugar: 2g, Protein: 9g

49. Vegan "Beef" Tacos

Taste the amazingness of vegan tacos with this delicious Vegan "Beef" Tacos recipe! Enjoy the savory flavors of the vegan beef-style crumbles and crunchy shells in these delicious tacos.

Serving: 4
Preparation Time: 10 minutes
Ready Time: 30 minutes

Ingredients:
- 1 (12-ounce) package vegan beef-style crumbles
- 2 tablespoons safflower oil
- 2 teaspoons chili powder
- 2 teaspoons ground cumin
- 1-15 ounce can black beans, drained and rinsed
- 1 cup vegan cheese
- 8 flour tortillas
- 2 cups shredded lettuce
- 1/2 cup salsa
- 2 tablespoons diced jalapeño (optional)

Instructions:
1. Preheat the oven to 350° F.
2. In a medium skillet, heat the safflower oil over medium-high heat.
3. Add the vegan beef-style crumbles and sauté for 5 minutes.
4. Add the chili powder, cumin, black beans, and salt and pepper to taste. Cook for an additional 5 minutes, stirring frequently.
5. Place the vegan cheese on the flour tortillas, and layer the vegan beef-style crumbles, lettuce, and salsa on top.
6. Place the filled tacos on a baking sheet and bake for 10 minutes.
7. Remove the tacos from the oven and top with the diced jalapeño (if desired).

Nutrition information:
Calories per Serving: 344, Total Fat: 15.6g, Saturated Fat: 3.7g, Polyunsaturated Fat: 8.8g, Monounsaturated:1.7g, Cholesterol: 0mg, Sodium: 1792mg, Potassium: 278mg, Carbohydrates: 42.1g, Fiber: 8.1g, Sugar: 1.7g, Protein: 12.3g

50. Jackfruit Banh Mi Sandwich

Jackfruit Banh Mi Sandwich is a delicious combination of vegan, Vietnamese flavors and classic sandwich Ingredients, served up on crunchy baguettes.
Serving: 4
Preparation time: 15 minutes
Ready time: 20 minutes

Ingredients:
- 2 cans jackfruit, drained
- 2 tablespoons vegetable oil
- 1/4 cup vegan fish sauce
- 2 tablespoons brown sugar
- 2 tablespoons lime juice
- 1 teaspoon garlic powder
- 1 teaspoon dried chili flakes
- 4 small baguettes
- 1/4 cup sliced pickled carrots
- 1/2 cup sliced cucumber
- 1/4 cup fresh cilantro leaves
- 1/4 cup vegan mayonnaise

Instructions:
1. Preheat a large sauté pan over medium heat. Once hot, add the drained jackfruit and oil.
2. Sauté for 5 minutes to soften the jackfruit, stirring occasionally.
3. In a small bowl, mix together the fish sauce, brown sugar, lime juice, garlic powder and chili flakes.
4. Pour into the hot pan and stir to coat the jackfruit.
5. Cook for an additional 5 minutes to reduce and thicken the sauce.
6. Cut the baguettes in half lengthwise and toast.
7. Spread the vegan mayonnaise onto both sides of the toasted baguettes.
8. Layer on the jackfruit, pickled carrots, cucumber and cilantro.
9. Serve immediately.

Nutrition information: per serving (1 sandwich): 332 calories, 19g fat, 35g carbohydrates, 5g protein.

51. Tempeh Bacon and Avocado Wrap

A savory and delicious vegan wrap made with tempeh bacon, creamy avocado, and crunchy lettuce, this Tempeh Bacon and Avocado Wrap is the perfect healthy lunch or snack!
Serving: 2
Preparation time: 10 minutes
Ready time: 20 minutes

Ingredients:
- 4 slices Tempeh Bacon
- 1 tablespoon coconut oil
- 1/2 avocado, sliced
- 1 lettuce leaf
- 2 tablespoons vegan mayonnaise
- 2 flour tortillas

Instructions:
1. Heat a skillet over medium heat and add the coconut oil.
2. Once the oil is hot, add the tempeh bacon and cook for 5-7 minutes, flipping halfway through, until it is lightly browned and crisp.
3. Meanwhile, spread the vegan mayonnaise onto the tortillas.
4. On one half of each tortillas, layer the lettuce, tempeh bacon, and avocado slices.
5. Fold the tortillas in half and place onto the skillet. Cook for 1-2 minutes per side, until golden brown and crispy.
6. Serve warm.

Nutrition information
Serving size: 1 wrap
Calories: 300
Fat: 16 g
Carbohydrates: 27 g
Protein: 9 g
Fiber: 6 g

52. BBQ "Chick'n" Quesadillas

A delicious twist on the classic quesadilla, BBQ "Chick'n" Quesadillas are cheesy and full of flavor. Perfect for any night of the week, you can easily whip up these quesadillas in the oven, on the stove top, or in the air fryer.

Serving: 4
Preparation time: 10 mins
Ready time: 15 mins

Ingredients:
- 4 burrito- sized tortillas
- 2 cups vegan BBQ "Chick'n" bites
- 2 cups shredded vegan cheese
- 1/4 teaspoon onion powder
- 1/4 teaspoon garlic powder
- 1/4 teaspoon paprika
- 1/4 teaspoon salt
- 2 tablespoons vegetable oil

Instructions:
1. Preheat oven to 375°F (190°C).
2. In a large mixing bowl, combine vegan BBQ "Chick'n" bites, shredded vegan cheese, onion powder, garlic powder, paprika, and salt and mix together until evenly combined.
3. Place tortillas on a baking sheet lined with parchment paper.
4. Divide the vegan BBQ "Chick'n" mixture evenly among the four tortillas. Fold the tortilla over and press firmly to seal the edges.
5. Brush each quesadilla with vegetable oil, this will help the quesadillas get golden and crisp.
6. Bake for 15 minutes, or until the quesadillas are golden and crisp.
7. Let cool for 5 minutes before cutting and serving.

Nutrition information
Calories: 357, Fat: 10.3g, Saturated Fat: 1.9g, Sodium: 990mg, Carbs: 35.9g, Fiber: 3.8g, Protein: 24.2g.

53. Buffalo Cauliflower Wrap

Enjoy this tasty vegetarian version of the classic buffalo wrap. Serve up Buffalo Cauliflower Wraps at your next party or enjoy as a light and flavor-filled meal.
Serving: Makes 2 wraps
Preparation Time: 10 minutes
Ready Time: 25 minutes

Ingredients:
- 2 large whole-wheat wraps
- 1 cup cooked cauliflower florets
- 1/2 cup Buffalo sauce
- 1/4 cup ranch dressing
- 2 tablespoon olive oil
- 1/4 cup chopped celery
- 1/4 cup diced red onion
- 1 tablespoon chopped fresh parsley

Instructions:
1. Preheat oven to 425 degrees.
2. Place cauliflower florets on a baking sheet and toss with olive oil.
3. Bake, stirring halfway through, until lightly browned and tender, about 20 minutes.
4. Transfer cauliflower to a bowl and toss with Buffalo sauce.
5. To assemble wraps: Place wraps on a plate. Spread ranch dressing on each wrap. Place cauliflower mixture onto wraps. Top with celery, red onion, and parsley.
6. Roll up wraps and cut in half. Serve.

Nutrition information: Calories: 244, Fat: 16g, Saturated fat: 3.5g, Cholesterol: 0mg, Sodium: 1208mg, Carbohydrates: 21g, Fiber: 4g, Sugar: 5g, Protein: 6g

54. Teriyaki Tofu Rice Bowl

A healthy and delicious flavor-packed Teriyaki Tofu Rice Bowl, made with simple Ingredients, is a perfect meal for any day of the week.
Serving: 2
Preparation time: 10 minutes

Ready time: 20 minutes

Ingredients:
- 2 tablespoons of sesame oil
- 2 cloves of garlic, minced
- 1 (14 ounce) package of extra-firm tofu, cut into cubes
- 1/2 cup of teriyaki sauce
- 2 cups of cooked white rice
- 2 teaspoons of rice vinegar
- 1/4 cup of sliced green onions
- Salt and pepper, to taste

Instructions:
1. Heat the sesame oil in a large skillet over medium heat.
2. Add the garlic and tofu cubes and cook for 3-4 minutes, stirring occasionally, until the tofu is golden and crispy.
3. Pour in the teriyaki sauce and stir until the tofu cubes are evenly coated.
4. In a bowl, mix the cooked white rice with the rice vinegar and green onions.
5. Add the tofu to the bowl and stir until evenly combined.
6. Top with salt and pepper, to taste.
7. Serve and enjoy!

Nutrition information:
Calories: 524 | Fat: 26g | Protein: 19g | Carbs: 51g | Sodium: 845mg

55. Vegan "Meatball" Stroganoff

This delicious and comforting vegan version of classic beef Stroganoff is packed full of flavor but uses soya mince to create vegan "meatballs" instead. Serve on top of cooked noodles or rice for an easy dinner the whole family will love.
Serving: Serves 4
Preparation Time: 10 minutes
Ready Time: 20 minutes

Ingredients:

- ½ cup cooked soya mince
- 2 tablespoons plain flour
- 2 tablespoons olive oil
- 1 onion, finely chopped
- 1 clove garlic, minced
- 200g white mushrooms, thinly sliced
- 2 tablespoons tomato paste
- ¼ cup vegan white wine (optional)
- 2 cups vegetable stock
- 2 tablespoons nutritional yeast flakes (optional)
- ¼ teaspoon smoked paprika
- 2 tablespoons vegan sour cream
- Salt and pepper to taste

Instructions:
1. In a bowl, mix together the soya mince, flour, and a pinch of salt and pepper until combined. Form into small "meatballs".
2. Heat the olive oil in a large skillet over medium heat. Add the onion and garlic and cook for a few minutes until softened.
3. Add the mushrooms and tomato paste to the skillet. Cook for a few more minutes, stirring occasionally.
4. Add the white wine (if using), vegetable stock, nutritional yeast flakes, smoked paprika and prepared "meatballs". Simmer for about 10 minutes, stirring from time to time.
5. Remove from heat and add the vegan sour cream. Stir to combine.
6. Serve the finished stroganoff with cooked noodles or rice.

Nutrition information: Per Serving: 339 calories; 11.9 g fat; 42.7 g carbohydrates; 15.1 g protein; 5.2 g fiber.

56. Smoky Chipotle Seitan Tacos

Smoky Chipotle Seitan Tacos are the perfect vegan taco recipe, loaded with smoky, spicy and flavourful seitan and topped off with crunchy salad and homemade chipotle mayo.
Serving: 4-6 servings
Preparation Time: 10 minutes
Ready Time: 40 minutes

Ingredients:
- 2 tablespoons of olive oil
- 2 red onion, sliced
- 2 red bell pepper, diced
- 2 cloves garlic, minced
- 2 tablespoons chili powder
- 2 teaspoon ground cumin
- 1 teaspoon smoked paprika
- 1 teaspoon chipotle powder
- 1 teaspoon oregano
- 1 teaspoon salt
- 1/4 teaspoon black pepper
- 2 cups cooked seitan
- 1/4 cup vegetable broth
- 8-10 soft tortillas
- 2 cups shredded lettuce
- 1 cup diced tomatoes
- 1 cup corn kernels
- 2 avocados, diced
- 1/4 cup chopped cilantro
- Chipotle mayonnaise, for serving

Instructions:
1. Heat the oil in a pan over medium heat.
2. Add the onion, bell pepper, garlic, chili powder, cumin, smoked paprika, chipotle powder, oregano, salt, and black pepper.
3. Cook for 4-5 minutes, stirring occasionally, until the vegetables are cooked and aromatic.
4. Add the seitan and stir for another 2 minutes.
5. Add the vegetable broth and stir for another 5 minutes until the seitan is cooked through.
6. Heat the tortillas according to the instructions on the package and assemble the tacos, dividing the cooked seitan among the tortillas.
7. Top with the lettuce, tomatoes, corn, avocados, and cilantro.
8. Serve with some chipotle mayo on the side.

Nutrition information: Per serving, Smoky Chipotle Seitan Tacos contains approximately 333 kcal, 19 g fat, 30 g carbohydrates, 10 g protein, and 6 g fiber.

57. Vegan "Chicken" and Waffle Sliders

Enjoy these vegan twist of classic southern chicken and waffle sliders. These hearty sliders are made with vegan chicken and waffle patties and served with a creamy maple syrup dressing.

Serving: 12 sliders
Preparation Time: 15 minutes
Ready Time: 30 minutes

Ingredients:
- 1 package vegan chicken-style strips
- 1 vegan pancake mix
- 1 teaspoon garlic powder
- 1 teaspoon onion powder
- 1/4 teaspoon black pepper
- 3 tablespoons oil
- 6 whole wheat hamburger buns, lightly toasted
- 1/4 cup vegan mayonnaise
- 2 teaspoon pure maple syrup

Instructions:
1. In a medium bowl, prepare the vegan pancake mixture according to the instructions.
2. In a separate bowl, mix together the vegan chicken-style strips, garlic powder, onion powder, and black pepper.
3. In a skillet, heat 2 tablespoons of oil on medium heat.
4. Take the prepared vegan chicken-style strips and carefully add them to the skillet. Cook for about 5 minutes, flipping the vegan chicken-style strips occasionally, until they're golden brown. Once they're ready, remove them from the heat.
5. Use a non-stick cooking spray to lightly coat a second skillet. Pour 1/2 of prepared pancake mixture into the skillet. Cook the vegan pancake for 5 minutes per side, or until both sides are golden.
6. To assemble the vegan chicken and waffle sliders, spread a tablespoon of vegan mayonnaise on each side of the lightly toasted hamburger buns. On one side of the bun, place the vegan chicken-style strips. On the

other side, place the vegan pancake. Top the vegan pancake with the vegan mayonnaise mixed with maple syrup.

Nutrition information:
Calories: 200, Fat: 9g, Saturated Fat: 3g, Cholesterol: 0mg, Sodium: 530mg, Carbohydrates: 24g, Fiber: 2g, Sugar: 7g, Protein: 7g

58. Spicy Buffalo Chickpea Salad

This tasty Spicy Buffalo Chickpea Salad is a great way to jazz up an otherwise ordinary salad. It features fresh bell peppers, celery, and chickpeas all mixed together and tossed in a spicy buffalo sauce. All that combined makes for a vibrant, flavorful, and nourishing dish that will make a great addition to your meal.
Serving: 6
Preparation Time: 10 minutes
Ready Time: 10 minutes

Ingredients:
1 15-ounce can chickpeas, drained and rinsed
1 red bell pepper, chopped
1 green bell pepper, chopped
1 stalk celery, chopped
3 tablespoons buffalo sauce
Salt and pepper, to taste

Instructions:
1. In a large bowl, combine the chickpeas, bell peppers, and celery.
2. Add the buffalo sauce and mix everything until evenly coated.
3. Add salt and pepper to taste and mix again.
4. Serve the salad immediately or chill until ready to serve.

Nutrition information: Per serving, this Spicy Buffalo Chickpea Salad contains approximately 151 calories, 5g fat, 24g carbohydrates, and 6g protein.

59. Vegan Gyro Bowl

Vegan Gyro Bowl is an indulgent and flavorful vegan alternative to traditional Gyro. It's filled with bold flavors and a variety of textures that you'll enjoy.
Serving: 4
Preparation time: 10 minutes
Ready time: 10 minutes

Ingredients:
- 1 package of Store Bought Vegan Gyro Meat (such as Beyond Meat or Impossible Gyro Meat
- 2 cups of cooked quinoa
- 1 red onion, diced
- 2 tomatoes, diced
- 1/4 cup of diced cucumber
- 1/4 cup of Kalamata olives, sliced
- 2 tablespoons of olive oil
- 2 tablespoons of apple cider vinegar
- 2 tablespoons of dried oregano
- Salt and pepper to taste

Instructions:
1. Preheat oven to 375°F and prepare a baking sheet.
2. Place vegan gyro meat on baking sheet and bake for 15 minutes, stirring occasionally.
3. Meanwhile, in a medium sized bowl, combine cooked quinoa, red onion, tomatoes, cucumber, and Kalamata olives.
4. In a small bowl, whisk together olive oil, apple cider vinegar, oregano, salt and pepper.
5. Pour over quinoa mixture and toss to combine.
6. Once the vegan gyro meat is finished baking, add to the quinoa bowl and mix well.
7. Divide the Vegan Gyro Bowl into 4 portions and serve.

Nutrition information (per serving): Calories: 310, Fat: 10g, Carbohydrates: 39g, Protein: 14g, Fiber: 7g, Sugar: 8g

60. BBQ Jackfruit Nachos

Enjoy the fresh taste of BBQ Jackfruit Nachos with this easy vegan recipe!
Serving: Serves 4
Preparation Time: 10 minutes
Ready Time: 20 minutes

Ingredients:
1 20-ounce can of young jackfruit, drained
1/2 cup vegan BBQ sauce
1 tablespoon avocado or olive oil
1 teaspoon smoked paprika
1 teaspoon garlic powder
1/2 teaspoon onion powder
1/2 teaspoon dried oregano
1/2 teaspoon ground cumin
1/2 teaspoon sea salt
Pepper to taste
1 large sweet potato, thinly sliced
1/2 large yellow bell pepper, finely diced
1/2 large red onion, finely diced
1 jalapeño pepper, thinly sliced
juice of 2 limes
4 ounces vegan cheese, finely grated
2 green onions, thinly sliced
1/2 cup fresh cilantro leaves, finely chopped

Instructions:
1. Preheat oven to 375°F.
2. Drain the jackfruit and add it to a large bowl. Use your hands or two forks to shred the jackfruit into bite-sized pieces, so it resembles pulled pork.
3. Add the BBQ sauce, oil, paprika, garlic powder, onion powder, oregano, cumin, and salt to the bowl, and stir to coat the jackfruit evenly.
4. Spread the jackfruit mixture onto an ungreased sheet pan. Bake in the preheated oven for 20 minutes.
5. While the jackfruit is cooking, assemble the nachos. To do this, spread the sweet potato slices, bell pepper, red onion, jalapeño, and lime juice over an oven-safe dish.

6. Top the dish with the shredded jackfruit, and sprinkle the vegan cheese, green onions, and cilantro on top.
7. Bake for 10 minutes, or until vegan cheese is melted and the vegetables are tender.

Nutrition information: Calories 225, Total Fat 6g, Saturated Fat 2g, Cholesterol 0mg, Sodium 354mg, Total Carbohydrate 37g, Dietary Fiber 6g, Total Sugars 15g, Protein 6g.

61. Vegan Breakfast Hash

Vegan Breakfast Hash is an easy and delicious meal packed with flavor and nutrition. It is made with a variety of vegetables, herbs, and seasonings, making it a perfect option to start your day!
Serving
Serves 4
Preparation Time
15 minutes
Ready Time
30 minutes

Ingredients:
- 1 tablespoon olive oil
- 1 small onion, diced
- 1 red pepper, diced
- 1 yellow pepper, diced
- 1 cup mushrooms, sliced
- 1 zucchini, diced
- 2 cloves garlic, minced
- 1 teaspoon dried oregano
- 1 teaspoon smoked paprika
- 1/4 teaspoon sea salt
- 1/2 teaspoon black pepper
- 1/2 teaspoon red pepper flakes, optional
- 4 cups cooked potatoes, cubed
- 1/4 cup fresh parsley, minced

Instructions:

1. Heat olive oil in a large skillet over medium-high heat.
2. Add onion, red pepper, yellow pepper, mushrooms, and zucchini. Saute for about 5 minutes or until vegetables are tender.
3. Add garlic, oregano, smoked paprika, sea salt, black pepper and red pepper flakes, if using. Cook until fragrant, about 30 seconds.
4. Add potatoes and cook, stirring often, for 5 minutes or until potatoes are hot and lightly browned.
5. Stir in parsley and cook until just wilted, about 1 minute.

Nutrition information
Calories: 143 kcal, Carbohydrates: 18 g, Protein: 3 g, Fat: 6 g, Saturated Fat: 1 g, Sodium: 168 mg, Potassium: 578 mg, Fiber: 3 g, Sugar: 3 g, Vitamin A: 1098 IU, Vitamin C: 46 mg, Calcium: 45 mg, Iron: 1 mg

62. Chickpea and Vegetable Stir Fry

This Chickpea and Vegetable Stir Fry is a flavorful and healthy vegan dish that can be ready in just 30 minutes! It's also great for meal prep.
Serving: 4-6
Preparation time: 10 minutes
Ready time: 20 minutes

Ingredients:
- 1 tablespoon olive oil
- 1 onion, diced
- 2 cloves garlic, minced
- 1 teaspoon ground cumin
- 1 teaspoon coriander
- 2 carrots, diced
- 1 red bell pepper, diced
- 1 cup frozen peas
- 2 cups cooked chickpeas
- 1/4 cup vegetable broth or water
- Salt and pepper to taste
- 2 tablespoons freshly chopped cilantro (optional)

Instructions:

1. Heat the olive oil in a large skillet over medium heat. Add the diced onion and cook for 5 minutes until softened.
2. Add the garlic, cumin and coriander and cook for an additional minute.
3. Add the diced carrots and bell pepper and cook for 5 minutes.
4. Add the frozen peas and cooked chickpeas and stir to combine.
5. Pour the vegetable broth or water over the vegetables and cook for 10 minutes until everything is cooked through. Season with salt and pepper to taste.
6. Remove from heat and stir in the chopped cilantro if using. Serve hot.

Nutrition information: Per serving (based on 6 servings): Calories: 176; Carbohydrates: 24g; Protein: 9g; Fat: 6g; Saturated fat: 1g; Sodium: 30mg; Fiber: 8g; Sugar: 4g.

63. Vegan "Beef" and Black Bean Burritos

Enjoy this hearty and nutritious vegan burrito with a blend of black beans and textured vegetable protein that tastes just like beef!
Serving: 2 burritos
Preparation time: 15 minutes
Ready time: 25 minutes

Ingredients:
- ½ cup textured vegetable protein
- ½ cup boiling water
- ½ teaspoon cumin
- ¾ teaspoon chili powder
- ¼ teaspoon garlic powder
- ½ teaspoon paprika
- 2 teaspoons olive oil
- ¼ cup onion, chopped
- ½ cup red bell pepper, chopped
- ½ cup black beans, cooked
- 2 burrito-size flour tortillas
- Chopped tomatoes, for garnish
- 2 tablespoons cilantro, chopped
- 2 tablespoons vegan cheese, shredded

Instructions:
1. In a small bowl, add the textured vegetable protein and boiling water. Let sit for 5 minutes then drain and set aside.
2. In a small bowl, mix together the cumin, chili powder, garlic powder, and paprika.
3. Heat the oil in a large skillet over medium heat. Add the onion and bell pepper and cook for 4 minutes.
4. Add the textured vegetable protein and the spices and cook until heated through, about 3-5 minutes.
5. Add the black beans and cook until heated through, about 3-5 minutes.
6. Warm the tortillas in the oven for a few minutes.
7. Divide the black bean mixture evenly between the two tortillas. Top with tomatoes, cilantro, and vegan cheese.
8. Roll the tortillas up and serve.

Nutrition information: Calories: 208, Total Fat: 6.4g, Saturated Fat: 1.3g, Sodium: 308mg, Carbohydrates: 29.7g, Fiber: 6.8g, Protein: 8.4g, Cholesterol: 0mg.

64. Jackfruit Curry

Jackfruit curry is a delicious and flavorful dish from Southern India that combines ripe jackfruit with spices and coconut milk. It's vegan, gluten-free and absolutely delicious.
Serving: 4
Preparation time: 15 minutes
Ready time: 30 minutes

Ingredients:
- 1 tablespoon cooking oil
- 1 teaspoon mustard seeds
- 1 teaspoon cumin seed
- 1 teaspoon coriander powder
- 4 fresh curry leaves
- 2 cups of diced ripe jackfruit
- 1 onion, chopped

- 1 teaspoon ginger garlic paste
- 1 green chili, finely chopped
- 1 teaspoon garam masala
- 1/2 teaspoon turmeric powder
- 1/2 teaspoon chili powder
- 1/2 cup coconut milk
- Salt to taste

Instructions:
1. Heat the oil in a large skillet over medium heat.
2. Add the mustard seeds and let them start to splutter.
3. Add the cumin seeds, curry leaves, onion, ginger garlic paste, and green chili.
4. Cook until the onion is lightly browned, about 10 minutes.
5. Add the jackfruit, garam masala, turmeric powder, chili powder, and salt.
6. Cook for 10 minutes.
7. Add the coconut milk and cook for another 10 minutes, stirring occasionally.
8. Serve hot over cooked rice or your favorite side dish.

Nutrition information:
Serving Size: 1 Serving: Calories: 216 kcal
Total Fat: 15 g
Saturated fat: 11 g
Cholesterol: 0 mg
Sodium: 117 mg
Total Carbohydrates: 19 g
Fiber: 3 g
Protein: 3 g
Sugars: 10 g

65. Tempeh Bacon Breakfast Sandwich

Introducing a flavorful twist to a classic breakfast sandwich – tempeh bacon breakfast sandwich! This vegan-friendly option is loaded with savory ingredients that will keep you full and energized for the day.
Serving: 1 sandwich

Preparation Time: 10 minutes
Ready Time: 10 minutes

Ingredients:
- 2 slices of toasted bread
- 2-3 slices of cooked tempeh bacon
- 1 vegan egg patty or your favorite vegan breakfast patty
- 1 slice of vegan cheese
- Shredded lettuce
- 2 tablespoons vegan mayonnaise

Instructions:
1. Prepare the tempeh bacon and vegan egg patty according to package directions.
2. Toast the bread.
3. Place a slice of cheese on each slice of toast.
4. Place the tempeh bacon on one slice.
5. Layer the vegan egg patty, shredded lettuce, and mayonnaise on the other slice of toast.
6. Put the two slices of toast together and press down.
7. Serve and enjoy!

Nutrition information: Calories: 500, Protein: 21 g, Fat: 28 g, Carbs: 34 g, Fiber: 6 g, Sodium: 795 mg

66. BBQ "Chick'n" Lettuce Wraps

Enjoy these simple yet tasty BBQ Chick'n Lettuce Wraps! They are a perfect mix of crunchy fruit, flavorful chicken, and an irresistible BBQ sauce that will make your taste-buds dance in flavor! Serve them as a light dinner, or in snack-sized portions to share with your friends.
Serving: 4-6
Preparation Time: 10 minutes
Ready Time: 10 minutes

Ingredients:
- 4 boneless skinless chicken breasts
- 2/3 cup barbecue sauce

- 1 tablespoon olive oil
- 1 teaspoon garlic powder
- 1 teaspoon smoked paprika
- 1 teaspoon oregano
- 6 large lettuce leaves
- 1 avocado, sliced
- 1/2 cup cherry tomatoes, halved
- 1/4 cup sliced red onion

Instructions:
1. In a medium bowl, combine BBQ sauce, olive oil, garlic powder, smoked paprika, oregano, and black pepper.
2. Add chicken breasts and coat with the BBQ mixture. Transfer to a greased baking sheet and bake at 400°F for 12-15 minutes or until chicken is cooked through.
3. Once chicken is cooked, let cool for 5 minutes before shredding.
4. To assemble the wraps, place a large lettuce leaf on each plate. In the center of each leaf, add some chicken, avocado, tomato, and red onion slices.
5. Drizzle with extra BBQ sauce and serve.

Nutrition information: Serving size: 1 wrap, Calories 126, Total Fat 8.6 g, Cholesterol 27 mg, Sodium 678 mg, Total Carbohydrates 5.2 g, Dietary Fiber 1 g, Protein 8.9 g

67. Buffalo Cauliflower Mac and Cheese

Give your classic mac and cheese a makeover with this vegan Buffalo Cauliflower Mac and Cheese recipe. This creamy, spicy, and flavor-packed vegan mac and cheese is a must for game-day eating!
Serving: 4
Preparation time: 15 minutes
Ready time: 45 minutes

Ingredients:
- 1 head of cauliflower, cut into small florets
- 1/4 cup vegan butter
- 1/4 cup all-purpose flour

- 3 cups vegan unsweetened almond milk
- 2 tablespoons nutritional yeast
- 1 tablespoon apple cider vinegar
- 1 tablespoon garlic powder
- Ground black pepper, to taste
- 1/2 teaspoon paprika
- 1/4 teaspoon ground turmeric
- 1/4 teaspoon ground cayenne pepper
- 1/3 cup vegan buffalo sauce

Instructions:
1. Preheat the oven to 350 °F (176 °C).
2. Melt the vegan butter in a pot over medium-low heat.
3. Whisk in the all-purpose flour until combined. Then, slowly add in the almond milk and whisk vigorously until it's completely combined and creamy.
4. Let the sauce simmer for 8-10 minutes until it is thickened.
5. Add in the nutritional yeast, apple cider vinegar, garlic powder, black pepper, paprika, turmeric, and cayenne pepper. Whisk until smooth.
6. Bring a large pot of salted water to a boil. Add the cauliflower florets and let them boil for 3-4 minutes. Then, drain and let the cauliflower cool.
7. Grease an oven-safe baking dish with vegan butter.
8. Add the cooked cauliflower and buffalo sauce into the baking dish. Stir until everything is evenly coated.
9. Pour the vegan cheese sauce over the cauliflower and stir until the florets are completely coated.
10. Bake the buffalo cauliflower mac and cheese in the preheated oven for 30 minutes or until golden brown.
11. Serve the buffalo cauliflower mac and cheese warm. Enjoy!

Nutrition information: Per serving: 299 kcal, Total Fat 19 g, Saturated Fat 10 g, Protein 13 g, Total Carbohydrates 20 g, Dietary Fiber 6 g, Sugars 5 g, Cholesterol 0 mg.

68. Teriyaki Tofu and Vegetable Skewers

This dish brings together a delicious mix of teriyaki-glazed tofu and vegetables by skewering them. Enjoy this quick and easy vegan meal that is sure to be a hit with the whole family!
Serving: Makes 4 skewers
Preparation Time: 10 minutes
Ready Time: 10 minutes

Ingredients:
- 4 bamboo skewers
- 4oz tofu, cubed
-1 bell pepper, chopped
-1 zucchini, chopped
-1 onion, sliced
-3 tablespoons teriyaki sauce

Instructions:
1. Preheat the oven to 350°F.
2. Place the bamboo skewers on a foil-lined baking sheet.
3. Arrange the tofu, bell pepper, zucchini, and onion onto the skewers.
4. Drizzle each skewer with teriyaki sauce.
5. Bake the skewers for 8-10 minutes or until the veggies are tender and the tofu is golden.
6. Serve and enjoy!

Nutrition information:
Per skewer: calories - 119, fat - 2.7g, carbs - 18.3g, protein - 6.3g.

69. Vegan "Meatball" Sub Salad

This vegan meal consists of salad with vegan "meatballs" – a delicious and healthy choice for lunch or dinner.
Serving: 4 servings
Preparation time: 10 minutes
Ready time: 30 minutes

Ingredients:
For the Salad:
• 4 cups of lettuce

- 2 tomatoes, chopped
- 1 red onion, chopped
- 1/2 cup of olives
- 1/2 cup of vegan cheese

For the "Meatballs":
- 1/2 cup of cooked quinoa
- 1/2 cup of cooked lentils
- 1/4 cup of diced onion
- 1 tablespoon of olive oil
- 1 teaspoon of garlic powder
- 1 teaspoon of Italian seasoning
- 1 tablespoon of nutritional yeast

Instructions:
1. Preheat oven to 375 degrees.
2. In a bowl, combine the quinoa, lentils, onion, olive oil, garlic powder, Italian seasoning and nutritional yeast. Mix until all Ingredients are combined.
3. Form the mixture into small meatballs and place on a baking sheet lined with parchment paper.
4. Bake for 25-30 minutes, or until cooked through.
5. While the vegan "meatballs" are cooking, prepare the salad. Toss together the lettuce, tomatoes, red onion and olives in a large bowl.
6. Once the vegan "meatballs" are done, add them to the salad.
7. Top with vegan cheese and serve.

Nutrition information:
Calories: 219; Protein: 9.8g; Fat: 8.8g; Carbs: 23.2g; Fiber: 5.7g; Sugar: 2.7g; Cholesterol: 0mg

70. Smoky Chipotle Tempeh Wrap

Smoky Chipotle Tempeh Wrap is a light and flavorful wrap filled with spicy and creamy components that come together to make a delicious vegetarian meal.
Serving: 4
Preparation time: 10 minutes
Ready time: 25 minutes

Ingredients:
- 8 oz. tempeh
- 1/4 cup mayonnaise
- 2 tsp chipotle paste
- 2 tsp smoked paprika
- 1 tsp garlic powder
- 1/2 tsp onion powder
- 1/4 tsp salt
- 1/4 tsp black pepper
- 2 green onions, thinly sliced
- 4 whole-wheat wraps
- 2 cups baby spinach leaves

Instructions:
1. Begin by boiling your tempeh for 10 minutes in a medium-sized pot of boiling water. Once it's cooked, remove it from the water and set aside.
2. In a medium-sized bowl, mix together the mayonnaise, chipotle paste, smoked paprika, garlic powder, onion powder, salt, and black pepper. Mix until combined.
3. Shred the tempeh into small pieces and add to the bowl with the mayonnaise mixture. Mix until the tempeh is well-coated with the mixture.
4. Slice the green onions and add to the bowl. Stir to combine.
5. Heat a skillet over medium heat and spray with cooking oil.
6. Place the wraps onto the skillet and cook until lightly toasted and crispy.
7. Take a wrap and spread the tempeh mixture onto it and top with some baby spinach leaves.
8. Fold the wrap and enjoy!

Nutrition information:
Calories: 465, Total Fat: 21g, Saturated Fat: 3g, Cholesterol: 5mg, Sodium: 476mg, Total Carbohydrate: 45g, Dietary Fiber: 5g, Sugars: 3g, Protein: 17g

71. Vegan "Chicken" Fried Rice

Vegan "Chicken" Fried Rice is the perfect meatless meal for those looking for a tasty vegan option. This vegan version of the classic fried rice dish is made with a plant-based "chicken" substitute, giving it the same satisfying texture and flavor without the need for actual poultry.
Serving: 4-5
Preparation time: 10 minutes
Ready time: 25 minutes

Ingredients:
- "Chicken" substitute (1 package)
- 2 tablespoons vegetable oil
- 1 teaspoon sesame oil
- 1 onion, diced
- 2 cloves garlic, minced
- 1 bell pepper, diced
- 2 carrots, diced
- 3 cups cooked white or brown rice
- 1/4 cup low-sodium soy sauce
- 2 tablespoons rice vinegar
- 2 tablespoons chili paste
- 2 tablespoons sesame seeds

Instructions:
1. Prepare the "chicken" substitute according to the instructions on the package.
2. Heat vegetable oil and sesame oil in a large skillet over medium-high heat.
3. Add onion, garlic, bell pepper, and carrots and sauté for 5 minutes until vegetables are softened.
4. Stir in the cooked "chicken" substitute and cooked rice.
5. Stir in soy sauce, rice vinegar, and chili paste.
6. Reduce heat to medium-low and cook for an additional 10 minutes, stirring occasionally.
7. Sprinkle with sesame seeds and serve.

Nutrition information (per 1 serving):
- Calories: 365
- Total Fat: 17g
- Sodium: 779mg
- Carbohydrates: 40g

- Protein: 14g

72. Coconut Curry Quinoa Salad

This Coconut Curry Quinoa Salad is a mouthwatering vegetarian dish that will leave you full and satisfied. With quinoa, beans, a delicious curry sauce, and plenty of fresh veggies, it's a nutritious and delicious way to enjoy a meal.
Serving: 4
Preparation time: 20 minutes
Ready time: 40 minutes

Ingredients:
-1 garlic clove, minced
-1 tablespoon fresh ginger, minced
-1 teaspoon ground cumin
-1 teaspoon ground coriander
-1 teaspoon garam masala
-1/4 teaspoon ground turmeric
-1/2 teaspoon sea salt
-1/4 teaspoon freshly ground black pepper
-1 can of coconut milk
-1/2 cup green lentils
-1/2 cup quinoa, rinsed
-3 tablespoons olive oil
-1 red onion, diced
-1 bell pepper, diced
-1 zucchini, diced
-1 head of broccoli, chopped
-1 cup frozen peas
-2 tablespoons fresh lime juice
-Optional: fresh cilantro , toasted coconut flakes, and/or cashews for garnish

Instructions:
1. In a small bowl, mix together the garlic, ginger, cumin, coriander, garam masala, turmeric, sea salt, and pepper.

2. In a medium saucepan over medium heat, heat the coconut milk until simmering.
3. Add the spice mixture and stir until combined.
4. Add the lentils and quinoa and stir to combine. Reduce heat to low, cover, and simmer for 18-20 minutes, or until the quinoa and lentils are cooked.
3. Meanwhile, heat the olive oil in a large skillet over medium heat. Add the onions, bell pepper, zucchini, and broccoli and cook for 8-10 minutes, or until the vegetables are soft and lightly browned. Remove from heat.
4. Add the cooked quinoa and lentils to the skillet with the vegetables. Add the peas and lime juice and stir until combined.
5. Serve with desired toppings.

Nutrition information: Serving size: 1/4 of recipe, Calories: 394, Total fat: 21.1 g, Saturated fat: 11.3 g, Cholesterol: 0 mg, Sodium: 231.8 mg, Total carbohydrate: 42.2 g, Dietary fiber: 9.3 g, Sugars: 7.3 g, Protein: 9.6 g.

73. Vegan Sausage and Spinach Stuffed Portobello Mushrooms

Vegan Sausage and Spinach Stuffed Portobello Mushrooms is an easy and flavorful vegan entrée that can be on your dinner table in under an hour.
Serving: 4
Preparation time: 15 minutes
Ready time: 45 minutes

Ingredients:
- 4 large portobello mushroom caps
- 1 teaspoon olive oil
- 1/2 onion, diced
- 1 garlic clove, minced
- 1/2 teaspoon red pepper flakes
- 2 vegan sausages
- 1 bell pepper, diced
- 2 cups fresh spinach

- 2/3 cup vegan mozzarella, grated
- Salt & pepper to taste

Instructions:
1. Preheat oven to 350 degrees Fahrenheit.
2. Remove the stems from the mushrooms and scrape out some of the gills with a spoon.
3. Heat the olive oil in a medium skillet over medium heat.
4. Add the onions, garlic, and red pepper flakes to the skillet and sauté for 5 minutes over medium heat.
5. Add the vegan sausages to the skillet and cook until heated through, about 5 minutes, stirring often.
6. Add the bell peppers and spinach to the skillet and sauté until the bell peppers are tender, about 3-4 minutes.
7. Divide the sausage mixture into four portions and place into the mushrooms.
8. Top with the shredded vegan mozzarella.
9. Place on a baking tray and bake for 25-30 minutes, until the mushrooms are tender.

Nutrition information:
Per Serving:
Calories: 246 kcal,
Carbohydrates: 16 g,
Protein: 14 g,
Fat: 15 g,
Saturated Fat: 4 g,
Sodium: 544 mg,
Potassium: 554 mg,
Fiber: 3 g,
Sugar: 5 g,
Vitamin A: 1534 IU,
Vitamin C: 43 mg,
Calcium: 57 mg,
Iron: 2 mg

74. BBQ Jackfruit Stuffed Sweet Potatoes

BBQ Jackfruit Stuffed Sweet Potatoes is a unique and delicious gluten-free recipe that makes a great main course or side dish. The jackfruit adds a wonderful texture, and this dish is packed with flavor from all the amazing Ingredients.

Serving: 4 servings
Preparation time: 20 minutes
Ready time: 40 minutes

Ingredients:
- 2 tbsps olive oil
- 1 onion, chopped
- 3 cloves garlic, minced
- 2 cans jackfruit, drained and shredded
- 2 tsps smoked paprika
- 1/2 tsp ground cumin
- 1 tsp garlic powder
- Salt and pepper, to taste
- 1 cup BBQ sauce
- 2 sweet potatoes, cooked and scooped out
- 2 tbsps vegan Parmesan cheese

Instructions:
1. Preheat oven to 375F.
2. In a large skillet, heat the olive oil over medium heat and add the onion and garlic. Sauté until the onion is translucent, about 5 minutes.
3. Add the shredded jackfruit to the skillet and season with the smoked paprika, cumin, garlic powder, salt, and pepper. Stir to combine and cook until the jackfruit is lightly browned and fragrant, about 8 more minutes.
4. Stir in the BBQ sauce and cook for 2 more minutes.
5. Spoon the jackfruit mixture into the scooped sweet potatoes.
6. Place the stuffed sweet potatoes onto a baking sheet and sprinkle the Parmesan cheese over top.
7. Bake for 20 minutes, or until hot and bubbly.

Nutrition information (per serving):
Calories: 351
Fat: 10g
Carbohydrates: 56g
Protein: 8g
Fiber: 5g

75. Buffalo Cauliflower Tacos

Buffalo Cauliflower Tacos is a perfect choice for anyone looking for a vegan option! This delicious recipe uses freshly roasted cauliflower to provide a tasty and spicy filling, while the warm tortillas give the meal some flavor and texture. The recipe is super easy to make and comes together in just a few simple steps.

Serving: Serves 4
Preparation Time: 5 minutes
Ready Time: 40 minutes

Ingredients:
- 1 head of cauliflower cut into florets
- 2 tablespoons of olive oil
- 4 tablespoons of hot sauce
- 1/2 teaspoon of garlic powder
- 1/2 teaspoon of onion powder
- 8 small flour tortillas
- 2 avocadoes, diced
- 2 tablespoons of cilantro, chopped

Instructions:
1. Preheat the oven to 400 degrees Fahrenheit.
2. Place the cauliflower florets on a baking sheet and toss with olive oil, hot sauce, garlic powder, and onion powder.
3. Roast in the preheated oven for 30-35 minutes or until cauliflower is crisp and lightly browned.
4. Heat the tortillas in a skillet over medium heat.
5. To assemble, fill each tortilla with the roasted cauliflower, diced avocado and cilantro.
6. Serve hot.

Nutrition information:
(Per Serving)
Calories: 213
Fat: 10.1 g
Carbohydrate: 28.3 g

Protein: 4.8 g

76. Teriyaki Tofu Noodle Stir Fry

A savory and delicious Teriyaki Tofu Noodle Stir Fry that comes together in just 20 minutes. This satisfying vegan meal is bursting with bold flavors, noodles, and veggies.
Serving: Serves 4
Preparation time: 10 minutes
Ready time: 20 minutes

Ingredients:
- 8 ounces thin brown rice noodles
- 2 tablespoons coconut oil
- 1 (14 ounces) package firm tofu, diced
- 2 cloves garlic, minced
- 1 red bell pepper, thinly sliced
- 2 cups broccoli florets
- 1/4 cup tamari
- 2 tablespoons pure maple syrup
- 2 tablespoons white wine vinegar
- 1 tablespoon toasted sesame oil
- 1 teaspoon sriracha sauce
- 2 tablespoons sesame seeds

Instructions:
1. Bring a pot of water to a boil. Cook the noodles according to the package instructions. Drain them and set aside.
2. Heat the coconut oil in a large skillet or wok over medium-high heat. Add the tofu and cook until golden brown and crispy, about 5 minutes.
3. Add the garlic and bell pepper to the skillet and cook for 1 minute.
4. Add the broccoli, tamari, maple syrup, vinegar, sesame oil, and sriracha to the pan. Stir to combine. Cook until the vegetables are tender, about 5 minutes.
5. Add the cooked noodles to the pan. Toss until everything is combined and heated through.
6. Serve the stir fry garnished with sesame seeds.

Nutrition information: Per serving: 350 Calories, 24g Fat, 34g Carbs, 17g Protein

77. Vegan "Beef" and Mushroom Pot Pie

Veggie lovers, rejoice! This vegan "beef" and mushroom pot pie is packed with flavour and nutrition, and is incredibly easy to make.
Serving: 6
Preparation time: 15 minutes
Ready time: 45 minutes

Ingredients:
- 2-3 tablespoons oil
- 2 cloves garlic, minced
- 2 onions, diced
- 1 package vegan beefless crumbles
- 2 cups mushrooms, sliced
- 2 tablespoons dried parsley
- 1 teaspoon garlic powder
- 1 teaspoon onion powder
- Salt and pepper to taste
- 1 cup frozen peas
- 3 cups vegetable broth
- 1/2 cup all-purpose flour
- 2-3 tablespoons vegan margarine
- 2 tablespoons nutritional yeast
- 1 (9-inch) pie crust

Instructions:
1. Preheat the oven to 400°F.
2. Heat the oil in a large skillet over medium-high heat. Add the garlic and onions and cook for 3-4 minutes, or until the onions are softened.
3. Add the vegan beefless crumbles, mushrooms, parsley, garlic powder, onion powder, salt, and pepper. Cook for 5-7 minutes, or until the mushrooms are softened.
4. Add the frozen peas and vegetable broth. Bring to a boil, then reduce the heat to low and simmer for 5 minutes.

5. In a small bowl, whisk together the all-purpose flour, vegan margarine, and nutritional yeast until a thick paste forms. Slowly add the paste to the skillet, stirring constantly until the mixture thickens.
6. Transfer the mixture to a 9-inch pie dish and top with a prepared pie crust. Cut slits in the crust and bake for 15-20 minutes, or until the crust is golden-brown.

Nutrition information:
Calories: 308; Fat: 16g; Carbs: 32g; Protein: 12g; Sodium: 867mg; Fiber: 4g.

78. Jackfruit Tostadas

Enjoy these tasty Jackfruit Tostadas with an amazing combination of flavors! They are topped with crunchy slaw, creamy chipotle sauce, and juicy jackfruit. This vegan dish is just as good as its non-vegan counterpart!
Serving: 2
Preparation time: 15 minutes
Ready time: 30 minutes

Ingredients:
- 2 tostada shells
- 1/4 head of red cabbage, thinly sliced
- Juice from 1/2 lime
- 1/2 teaspoon salt
- 1/4 teaspoon black pepper
- 1/4 teaspoon garlic powder
- 1/4 cup vegan mayo
- 1 tablespoon chipotle hot sauce
- 1/4 teaspoon cumin
- 1/4 teaspoon smoked paprika
- 1/4 teaspoon garlic powder
- 1 (14 oz.) can of jackfruit, drained
- 2 tablespoons olive oil

Instructions:

1. Preheat the oven to 375F. Place the tostada shells on a greased baking sheet and bake for 10 minutes, flipping them after 5 minutes.
2. Meanwhile, in a medium bowl, mix together the sliced cabbage, juice from half a lime, salt, pepper, garlic powder. Set aside.
3. In a small bowl, mix together the vegan mayo, chipotle hot sauce, cumin, smoked paprika, garlic powder. Set aside.
4. In a medium skillet over medium heat, add jackfruit and olive oil. Sauté for about 5 minutes, stirring often.
5. Add the chipotle mayo mixture to the jackfruit and mix well. Cook for an additional 5 minutes, stirring often.
6. Remove the tostada shells from the oven and top with the cabbage mixture, followed by the jackfruit mixture.
7. Serve immediately.

Nutrition information: (per serving) Calories: 386; Fat: 21g; Carbs: 38g; Protein: 5g; Sodium: 732mg

79. Tempeh Bacon and Egg Breakfast Burrito

This hearty Tempeh Bacon and Egg Breakfast Burrito is packed with flavor and is a great way to start your day! It's high in protein and makes a delicious and satisfying meal.
Serving: Makes 2 burritos
Preparation Time: 10 minutes
Ready Time: 20 minutes

Ingredients:
- 2 tablespoons olive oil
- 8 ounces tempeh bacon, sliced
- 2 bell peppers, diced
- 1 small onion, diced
- 4 large eggs
- 1/4 teaspoon chili powder
- 1/4 teaspoon garlic powder
- 2 tablespoons chopped fresh cilantro
- 2 tortillas
- 2 tablespoons vegan mayonnaise
- Hot sauce, to taste

Instructions:
1. Heat the olive oil in a large skillet over medium heat. Add the tempeh bacon and cook, stirring occasionally, until browned and crisp, about 5 minutes.
2. Add the bell peppers and onion and cook until softened, about 5 minutes more.
3. Push the vegetables to one side of the pan and add the eggs. Sprinkle with the chili powder, garlic powder, and cilantro. Cook, stirring occasionally, until the eggs are scrambled and cooked through, about 5 minutes.
4. Meanwhile, warm the tortillas in the microwave or oven.
5. To assemble the burritos, spread a tablespoon of mayo on each tortilla. Add half of the egg mixture to each tortilla and top with hot sauce, if using. Roll up and serve.

Nutrition information: Vitamin A 9%, Calcium 4%, Vitamin C 46%, Iron 13%, 395 calories per burrito, 19 grams protein, 24 grams fat, 33 grams carbohydrates

80. BBQ "Chick'n" Lettuce Cups

These BBQ "Chick'n" Lettuce Cups make for a great light dinner or appetizer. This vegan-friendly dish combines plant-based proteins, crunchy lettuces, and sweet BBQ sauce for a complex flavor combination.
Serving: Makes 8 cups
Preparation time: 10 minutes
Ready time: 15 minutes

Ingredients:
- 1 package Gardein Chick'n Strips
- 1/4 cup BBQ sauce
- 1/4 cup diced red onion
- 1/4 cup diced fresh pineapple
- 8 lettuce cups
- Salt and pepper to taste

Instructions:
1. Preheat an oven to 375°F.
2. Spread out the Gardein Chick'n Strips on a baking sheet. Bake for 8-10 minutes until crispy and heated through.
3. While the Chick'n Strips are baking, mix together the BBQ sauce, red onion, and pineapple in a small bowl.
4. When the Chick'n Strips are finished baking, transfer them to a large bowl and add the BBQ sauce mixture. Stir until everything is combined.
5. Place a couple of tablespoons of the mixture into each lettuce cup. Serve immediately.

Nutrition information
- Calories: 90
- Fat: 1.5g
- Carbs: 14g
- Fiber: 2g
- Protein: 6g

81. Spicy Buffalo Chickpea Wraps

Spicy Buffalo Chickpea Wraps are a delicious plant-based meal made with flavorful and spicy chickpeas, creamy plant-based yogurt, and fresh vegetables rolled up in a wrap. Perfect for lunch, dinner, or a snack on the go!
Serving: Serves 4
Preparation time: 10 minutes
Ready time: 10 minutes

Ingredients:
- 1 can chickpeas, drained and rinsed
- 2 tablespoons buffalo sauce
- 2 tablespoons olive oil
- ½ teaspoon garlic powder
- ¼ teaspoon smoked paprika
- 2 whole wheat wraps
- 2 tablespoons plant-based yogurt
- 2 handfuls fresh spinach
- 2 tomatoes, diced

- 1/2 cup cooked quinoa (Optional)

Instructions:
1. Preheat the oven to 375°F.
2. Place the chickpeas in a bowl and mix with buffalo sauce, olive oil, garlic powder, and smoked paprika.
3. Spread the mixture evenly onto a baking sheet and bake for 8-10 minutes.
4. Heat the wraps in the oven for 3-5 minutes.
5. Remove the wraps from the oven and top each with plant-based yogurt and a layer of spinach.
6. Evenly sprinkle the chickpea mixture, tomatoes, and quinoa over the spinach.
7. Fold the wraps up and enjoy!

Nutrition information:
Calories: 364
Total Fat: 20g
Carbohydrates: 35g
Protein: 11g
Sodium: 891mg

82. Vegan Gyro Pita Pockets

These vegan gyro pita pockets pack a tasty punch! Filled with roasted veggies, dressed with tangy tzatziki sauce, and rolled in warm pita bread, this is a vegan delight that everyone can enjoy.
Serving: 4
Preparation Time: 20 minutes
Ready Time: 30 minutes

Ingredients:
- 2 tablespoons olive oil
- 2 cups chopped mushrooms
- ½ teaspoon garlic powder
- ¼ teaspoon smoked paprika
- 2 cups finely chopped cauliflower
- 1 teaspoon oregano

- Salt and pepper to taste
- 4 pieces of pita bread
- 1 cup vegan tzatziki sauce

Instructions:
1. Preheat the oven to 400°F. Line a baking sheet with foil.
2. In a large bowl, mix together the olive oil, mushrooms, garlic powder, smoked paprika, cauliflower, oregano, and salt and pepper to taste.
3. Spread the mixture onto the prepared baking sheet and bake for 20 minutes, stirring halfway through.
4. Heat the pita breads in the oven for 5 minutes.
5. To assemble, spread one tablespoon of tzatziki sauce onto each pita. Top with the roasted vegetable mixture and fold into a pocket.

Nutrition information: Per serving: 330 calories; 13g fat; 44g carbohydrates; 10g protein.

83. Vegan "Meatball" Stuffed Bell Peppers

Vegan "Meatball" Stuffed Bell Peppers are a delicious meatless meal that is hearty, flavorful, and incredibly satisfying.
Serving: 4
Preparation time: 15 minutes
Ready time: 45 minutes

Ingredients:
- 4 bell peppers
- 1 tablespoon olive oil
- 1 yellow onion, diced
- 4 cloves garlic, minced
- 2 cups mushrooms, diced
- 2 15-ounce cans chickpeas, drained and rinsed
- 1 heaping cup packed fresh parsley, chopped
- 3/4 teaspoon sea salt (plus more to taste)
- Freshly ground black pepper, to taste
- 1/4 teaspoon each: ground sage, thyme, oregano, and smoked paprika
- 2 tablespoons tomato paste
- 2 tablespoons nutritional yeast

- 2 tablespoons lemon juice

Instructions:
1. Preheat oven to 375 degrees F (190 C) and lightly oil a baking dish (I recommend 9×13).
2. Cut bell peppers in half lengthwise and remove tops and insides then place peppers cut side up in the baking dish.
3. Heat oil in a large skillet over medium heat. Once hot, add onion and garlic and sauté until lightly golden.
4. Add mushrooms and cook until soft and beginning to brown.
5. Transfer mixture to a large bowl.
6. Add drained chickpeas, parsley, salt, pepper, sage, thyme, oregano, and smoked paprika. Using a fork or potato masher, mash the chickpeas slightly.
7. Add tomato paste, nutritional yeast, and lemon juice and mix to combine.
8. Divide the filling mixture between the peppers, stuffing them as full as desired.
9. Cover the baking dish with foil then bake for 30 minutes.
10. Remove foil and bake uncovered for another 15 minutes or so, until lightly golden on top.
11. Serve and enjoy!

Nutrition information:
Calories: 351, Fat: 9 g, Carbohydrate: 50 g, Dietary Fiber: 13 g, Protein: 16 g

84. Smoky Chipotle Seitan Burger

This smoky and spicy vegan burger will tantalize your taste buds and fill you up! This delicious variation of an original vegan burger is made with seitan, chipotle peppers and a bunch of spices.
Serving: Makes two burgers
Preparation Time: 15 minutes
Ready Time: 25 minutes

Ingredients:
- 8 ounces seitan, cut into slices

- 1 tablespoon olive oil
- 2 teaspoons ground chipotle pepper
- 1 teaspoon smoked paprika
- 1 teaspoon oregano
- 1 teaspoon garlic powder
- 1 teaspoon onion powder
- 2 tablespoons tomato paste
- 2 hamburger buns
- 1 avocado, sliced
- 2 lettuce leaves
- 1 tomato, sliced

Instructions:
1. Preheat oven to 375°F.
2. In a small bowl, mix together the chipotle pepper, smoked paprika, oregano, garlic powder, and onion powder.
3. Place the seitan slices on a baking sheet lined with parchment paper.
4. Drizzle with the olive oil and sprinkle the spice mixture over the slices.
5. Bake for 10 minutes.
6. Spread the tomato paste over the slices and bake for an additional 10 minutes.
7. Heat a skillet over medium heat and cook the seitan slices for 3 minutes per side.
8. Assemble the burgers by placing the sliced avocados and lettuce leaves on the bottom bun. Top with the sliced tomatoes and seitan. Place the top bun on top and serve.

Nutrition information:
Calories: 253, Fat: 9g, Protein: 27g, Carbohydrates: 19g, Fiber: 5g, Sugar: 2g, Sodium: 314mg

85. Coconut Curry Lentil Buddha Bowl

Coconut Curry Lentil Buddha Bowl is a delicious vegan and gluten-free meal that is packed with flavor and texture. It is made with cooked lentils, fresh vegetables, and a creamy coconut curry sauce.
Serving: 4
Preparation time: 15 minutes

Ready time: 45 minutes

Ingredients:
- 1.5 cups dry lentils
- 2 tablespoons olive oil
- 1 small yellow onion, diced
- 3 cloves garlic, minced
- 1 red bell pepper, diced small
- 1 yellow bell pepper, diced small
- 1 large carrot, diced small
- 2 tablespoons curry powder
- 1 teaspoon ground cumin
- 1 teaspoon ground turmeric
- 1/2 teaspoon cayenne pepper
- 1/2 teaspoon ground coriander
- 1 can (14 oz) coconut milk
- 1/4 cup lime juice
- 2 teaspoons sea salt
- Freshly ground black pepper, to taste
- 2 cups cooked brown or white rice, for Serving: - Chopped fresh cilantro, for garnish

Instructions:
1. In a medium saucepan, cook the lentils according to package instructions. Drain and set aside.
2. Heat the olive oil in a large skillet over medium heat. Add the onion and garlic and sauté until softened, about 5 minutes.
3. Add the bell peppers and carrot and sauté for another 5 minutes.
4. Add the curry powder, cumin, turmeric, cayenne, and coriander and mix everything together.
5. Pour in the coconut milk and stir to combine. Bring to a simmer and let cook for 10 minutes.
6. Stir in the cooked lentils and lime juice, and season with salt and pepper. Simmer the curry for another 5 minutes, or until desired consistency is reached.
7. Serve over cooked brown or white rice with a sprinkle of chopped fresh cilantro.

Nutrition information:

Calories: 285; Total Fat: 15g; Cholesterol: 0mg; Sodium: 760mg; Total Carbohydrates: 29g; Dietary Fiber: 7g; Protein: 9g.

86. Vegan Sausage Breakfast Tacos

These delicious Vegan Sausage Breakfast Tacos are made with a flavorful combination of vegan sausage, tofu, bell peppers, onion, and spices. Packed with protein and flavor, they'll start your day off right!
Serving: 8 tacos
Preparation time: 10 minutes
Ready time: 25 minutes

Ingredients:
- 8 vegan sausages
- 2 tablespoons olive oil
- 1 (14-ounce) package extra-firm tofu, drained and pressed
- 1 red bell pepper, diced
- 1 yellow bell pepper, diced
- 1 white onion, diced
- 2 cloves garlic, minced
- 1 teaspoon smoked paprika
- 1/2 teaspoon chili powder
- 1/2 teaspoon garlic powder
- 1/2 teaspoon onion powder
- 1/2 teaspoon ground cumin
- 1/4 teaspoon ground black pepper
- 8 (6-inch) soft taco shells

Instructions:
1. Preheat the oven to 350°F. Place the vegan sausages on a parchment paper-lined baking sheet and bake for 20 minutes, flipping halfway through.
2. Meanwhile, heat the olive oil in a large skillet over medium heat. Add the tofu, bell peppers, onion, and garlic.
3. Cook for 7-10 minutes, stirring often, until the vegetables are softened.
4. Add the smoked paprika, chili powder, garlic powder, onion powder, cumin, and black pepper. Cook for 2 minutes, stirring occasionally.

5. Once the sausages are done, slice them into small pieces and add to the skillet with the vegetables.
6. Cook for 5-7 minutes, stirring often, until the sausages are warmed through.
7. Divide the filling among the taco shells.

Nutrition information: Per Serving (1 taco):
Calories: 264 kcal, Carbohydrates: 21 g, Protein: 11 g, Fat: 15 g, Saturated Fat: 4 g, Sodium: 465 mg, Potassium: 239 mg, Fiber: 3 g, Sugar: 2 g, Vitamin A: 698 IU, Vitamin C: 37 mg, Calcium: 60 mg, Iron: 2 mg

87. Vegan "Beef" and Quinoa Stuffed Bell Peppers

This vegan take on the classic 'beef' and quinoa stuffed bell peppers recipe is sure to please everyone! Packed with nourishing Ingredients, it's an easy and healthy meal that is sure to satisfy.
Serving: 4
Preparation time: 15 minutes
Ready time: 40 minutes

Ingredients:
- 4 bell peppers, preferably large
- 1/2 onion, diced
- 2 cloves garlic, minced
- 2 tablespoons olive oil
- 1 cup vegan ground 'beef'
- 1 teaspoon smoked paprika
- 1/2 teaspoon chili powder
- 1/2 teaspoon cumin
- 2 tablespoons tomato paste
- 2/3 cup cooked quinoa
- 1/2 vegetarian broth
- 1/3 cup black beans, rinsed
- 1/4 cup fresh parsley, chopped
- Salt and pepper to taste
- 1/2 cup vegan cheese (optional)

Instructions:

1. Preheat oven to 375F.
2. Cut the bell peppers in half, lengthwise, and discard the seeds and membranes.
3. Place peppers in a baking dish and set aside.
4. In a large sauté pan, add olive oil, onion, and garlic. Cook for 5-6 minutes until softened.
5. Add vegan beef, smoked paprika, chili powder, and cumin. Cook for 5-7 more minutes until vegan beef is cooked through.
6. Add tomato paste, cooked quinoa, vegetarian broth, black beans, and parsley. Cook for 3-5 minutes until tomato paste is fully mixed in.
7. Taste and adjust seasonings with salt and pepper as desired.
8. Fill each bell pepper half with the vegan beef and quinoa mixture. Top with vegan cheese, if desired.
9. Bake in preheated oven for 25-30 minutes until bell peppers are soft.
10. Serve immediately.

Nutrition information:
Calories: 284
Fat: 10 g
Carbohydrates: 28 g
Protein: 15 g
Fiber: 8 g

88. Jackfruit Chili

Jackfruit Chili is a delicious, sweet and savory dish that is perfect for a weekend dinner. The combination of spices, vegetables, and jackfruit makes for a unique and flavorful dish that will impress your family and friends.
Serving: 4-6
Preparation Time: 20 minutes
Ready Time: 40 minutes

Ingredients:
- 2 cans of jackfruit (in brine, drained)
- 1 can of black beans, rinsed
- 1 red onion, diced
- 1 red bell pepper, diced

- 2 cloves of garlic, minced
- 1 teaspoon ground cumin
- 2 tablespoons Chili powder
- 2 teaspoons smoked paprika
- 1 teaspoon oregano
- 1/2 teaspoon cayenne pepper
- 2 cups vegetable broth
- 1 lime, 2 tablespoons juice
- Salt and black pepper to taste

Instructions:
1. Heat 1 tablespoon of oil in a large pot over medium-high heat.
2. Add the onion and bell pepper to the pot and sauté for 5 minutes until the vegetables are soft and lightly browned.
3. Add garlic and jackfruit, breaking up the jackfruit with your spoon into small pieces.
4. Add the spices, including cumin, chili powder, smoked paprika, oregano, cayenne pepper, salt, and pepper. Stir for 1-2 minutes.
5. Add the black beans, vegetable broth, and lime juice. Bring to a simmer.
6. Lower the heat and simmer, partially covered, for 25-30 minutes until the jackfruit is tender.
7. Taste and adjust seasonings if needed.

Nutrition information: Per Serving: 230 calories; 7.6g fat; 31.6g carbohydrates; 7.3g protein

89. Teriyaki Tofu and Broccoli Stir Fry

This delicious stir fry is an easy and healthy weeknight dinner that will be on the table in less than 30 minutes. It is packed with protein from the tofu and nutritional value from the broccoli.
Serving: 4
Preparation Time: 10 minutes
Ready Time: 20 minutes

Ingredients:
- 2 tablespoons tamari (or soy sauce)

- 1 tablespoon rice vinegar
- 1 tablespoon honey
- 1 tablespoon sesame oil
- 2 cloves minced garlic
- 2 tablespoons chopped fresh ginger
- 14 ounces extra-firm tofu, drained and pressed
- 1 bunch broccoli florets
- 3 tablespoons vegetable oil, divided
- 1/4 teaspoon red pepper flakes
- 2 scallions, thinly sliced

Instructions:

1. In a small bowl, whisk together the tamari, rice vinegar, honey, sesame oil, garlic, and ginger; set aside.
2. Cut the tofu into 1/2-inch pieces.
3. In a large skillet or wok over medium-high heat, heat 2 tablespoons of vegetable oil.
4. Add the tofu and cook for 5 minutes, until golden and slightly crisp.
5. Remove the tofu from the skillet and set aside on a plate.
6. Add the remaining tablespoon of vegetable oil to the skillet and heat over medium-high heat.
7. Add the broccoli florets and cook for 3 minutes, stirring occasionally.
8. Add the red pepper flakes and the reserved tofu and stir to combine.
9. Add the reserved tamari mixture and cook everything for 2 minutes, until the broccoli is tender.
10. Garnish with scallions to serve.

Nutrition information:
Calories: 307 kcal, Carbohydrates: 14 g, Protein: 15 g, Fat: 20 g, Saturated Fat: 3 g, Sodium: 576 mg, Potassium: 375 mg, Fiber: 2 g, Sugar: 5 g, Vitamin C: 36 mg, Calcium: 308 mg, Iron: 2 mg

90. BBQ "Chick'n" Flatbread

BBQ 'Chick'n' Flatbread is a simple, delicious, and convenient meal that is easy to throw together in under 30 minutes! It's a crowd pleaser as it features a combination of flavors that everyone will love.
Serving: Makes 4 flatbreads.
Preparation time: 15 minutes
Ready time: 15 minutes

Ingredients:
- 2 tablespoons olive oil
- BBQ sauce
- 1 cup cooked and shredded chicken
- 4 flatbreads
- 1/2 cup of your favorite shredded cheese
- 2 tablespoons of your favorite chopped fresh herbs

Instructions:
1. Preheat the oven to 350°F.
2. Drizzle olive oil over the baking sheet and place the four flatbreads on top. Spread a tablespoon of BBQ sauce on each flatbread.
3. Top with shredded chicken and cheese. Sprinkle with the fresh herbs.
4. Bake in the preheated oven for 10-12 minutes, or until flatbread is golden brown and cheese is melted.
5. Enjoy!

Nutrition information: Serving size: 1 flatbread, Calories: 320, Fat: 15g, Saturated fat: 5g, Cholesterol: 50mg, Sodium: 600mg, Carbohydrates: 37g, Fiber: 2g, Protein: 13g.

91. Buffalo Cauliflower Salad Bowl

Buffalo Cauliflower Salad Bowl is an easy yet flavorful vegan salad that is packed with nutrients from cauliflower and a creamy homemade dressing. It's delicious and requires only a few Ingredients, making it perfect for a quick lunch to serve for a crowd.
Serving: 4-6
Preparation time: 10 minutes
Ready time: 15 minutes

Ingredients:
- 1 cauliflower head, chopped into florets
- 2 tablespoons olive oil
- Salt and pepper to taste
- 1/2 cup buffalo sauce
- 2 tablespoons vegan mayo
- 2 tablespoons vegan yogurt
- 1 tablespoon apple cider vinegar
- 2 green onions, chopped
- 2 tablespoons chopped cilantro
- 1/2 cup sliced olives

Instructions:
1. Preheat oven to 425°F. Line a large baking sheet with parchment paper.
2. Place cauliflower florets on the baking sheet and drizzle with olive oil. Sprinkle with salt and pepper.
3. Bake for 15 minutes, stirring halfway through.
4. In a bowl, mix together buffalo sauce, mayo, yogurt, and apple cider vinegar until combined.
5. Once the cauliflower is done baking, remove it from the oven and add it to the bowl. Stir until the cauliflower is evenly coated in the sauce.
6. Add the green onions, cilantro, and olives and mix until combined.
7. Serve warm or at room temperature.

Nutrition information:
Serving size: 1 bowl
Calories: 142; Total fat: 12g; Saturated fat: 2g; Cholesterol: 0mg; Carbohydrate: 6.8g; Dietary fiber: 2.5g; Protein: 2.3g; Sodium: 851mg

92. Tempeh Bacon and Avocado Toast

This Tempeh Bacon and Avocado Toast is perfect for a savory breakfast or brunch! It's a vegan and gluten-free dish, packed with plant-based flavor and nutrients.
Serving: 4
Preparation time: 10 minutes
Ready time: 10 minutes

Ingredients:
- 4 strips tempeh bacon
- 2-3 tablespoons olive oil
- 1/4 teaspoon garlic powder
- 1/4 teaspoon smoked paprika
- 4 slices sourdough bread
- 4 tablespoons guacamole
- 1 cup cherry tomatoes, halved
- 2 avocados, sliced

Instructions:
1. Preheat your oven to 375°F.
2. Place the tempeh bacon strips on a lined baking tray. Drizzle with olive oil, garlic powder, and smoked paprika.
3. Bake for 10 minutes.
4. Toast the sourdough bread.
5. Spread each slice with one tablespoon of guacamole.
6. Top with tomatoes, avocado slices, and tempeh bacon.

Nutrition information:
- Calories: 360 kcal
- Carbohydrates: 34 g
- Protein: 14 g
- Fat: 20 g
- Saturated Fat: 2 g
- Sodium: 440 mg
- Potassium: 735 mg
- Fiber: 7 g
- Sugar: 2 g
- Vitamin A: 370 IU
- Vitamin C: 14 mg
- Calcium: 82 mg
- Iron: 2.3 mg

93. Vegan "Chicken" Pad Thai

Get ready to try the most delicious vegan "Chicken" Pad Thai that you'll ever taste! This recipe adds fragrant and savory flavors for an unforgettable meal.

Serving: 2-3
Preparation Time: 35 minutes
Ready Time: 40 minutes

Ingredients:
- 1 package vegan "chicken"
- 2 tablespoons vegetable oil
- 2 tablespoons lime juice
- 2 tablespoons soy sauce
- 2 tablespoons brown sugar
- 1 tablespoon Sriracha
- 1 teaspoon ground ginger
- 2 cloves garlic, minced
- 2 tablespoons chopped peanuts
- 2 cups cooked rice noodles
- 2 tablespoons chopped cilantro

Instructions:
1. In a small bowl, mix together lime juice, soy sauce, brown sugar, Sriracha, and ground ginger.
2. Heat a wok or large skillet over medium-high heat. Once hot, add oil and vegan "chicken". Sauté for 2-3 minutes, until beginning to brown.
3. Add garlic to skillet and sauté for an additional minute.
4. Add sauce and cooked rice noodles. Continue to stir-fry for another 3-5 minutes.
5. Add chopped peanuts, cilantro, and additional sauce, to taste.
6. Serve hot and enjoy!

Nutrition information:
Calories: 640, Total Fat: 22g, Saturated Fat: 11g, Trans Fat: 0g, Cholesterol: 0mg, Sodium: 898mg, Carbohydrates: 90g, Fiber: 3g, Sugar: 16g, Protein: 18g

94. Chickpea and Vegetable Coconut Curry

This Chickpea and Vegetable Coconut Curry is an exquisite blend of mild flavors and fragrant spices, creating a delicious and nutritious vegan or vegetarian meal.

Serving: 4
Preparation Time: 10 minutes
Ready Time: 40 minutes

Ingredients:
- 1 tablespoon olive oil
- 1 onion, chopped
- 1/2 teaspoon ground ginger
- 1 teaspoon ground cumin
- 1/2 teaspoon ground coriander
- 1/4 teaspoon turmeric
- 2 cloves garlic, minced
- 2 carrots, chopped
- 2 cups cooked chickpeas
- 1 (14 ounce) can coconut milk
- 1 (14.5 ounce) can diced tomatoes, undrained
- 1/2 cup chopped fresh cilantro
- 2 cups cooked basmati rice

Instructions:
1. Heat the oil in a large skillet over medium-high heat.
2. Add the onion and sauté for about 3 minutes, until softened.
3. Add the ginger, cumin, coriander, and turmeric and cook for 1 minute, stirring frequently.
4. Add the garlic and carrots and cook for another minute, stirring frequently.
5. Add the chickpeas, coconut milk, and tomatoes and bring to a simmer.
6. Simmer for 15-20 minutes, stirring occasionally, until the sauce thickens.
7. Add the cilantro and stir to combine.
8. Serve over cooked basmati rice.

Nutrition information:
Calories: 476, Fat: 25g, Protein: 13g, Carbohydrates: 51g, Fiber: 9g, Sugars: 6g, Sodium: 310mg

95. Vegan "Meatball" and Veggie Skewers

Enjoy this delicious vegan alternative to a classic Italian dish with vegan "meatball" and veggie skewers. This recipe is easy to make with no added oil, full of protein and dietary fiber, and bursting with flavor.
Serving: 4
Preparation Time: 10 minutes
Ready Time: 25 minutes

Ingredients:
- 1/2 cup cooked quinoa
- 1/2 cup cooked red lentils
- 2 tablespoons tomato paste
- 1 teaspoon garlic powder
- 1 teaspoon oregano
- 1 teaspoon cumin
- Salt & pepper, to taste
- 2 portabello mushrooms, sliced
- 1/2 zucchini, sliced
- 1 bell pepper, sliced

Instructions:
1. Preheat the oven to 425 degrees F.
2. In a food processor or blender, combine the cooked quinoa and lentils with the tomato paste, garlic powder, oregano, cumin, salt and pepper. Process until combined and form into 16 small balls.
3. Place "meatballs" and vegetables on 4 skewers.
4. Bake in the preheated oven for 15 minutes.
5. Serve and enjoy!

Nutrition information (per serving):
Calories: 220
Fat: 2 g
Carbohydrates: 33 g
Protein: 12 g
Fiber: 10 g
Sugar: 5 g
Sodium: 200 mg

96. Smoky Chipotle Tempeh Lettuce Wraps

Enjoy a unique and delicious vegan meal with these Smoky Chipotle Tempeh Lettuce Wraps. Packed with flavor from smoked paprika, chipotle peppers, and garlic, these wraps are sure to leave you wanting more.

Serving: 4
Preparation Time: 15 minutes
Ready Time: 15 minutes

Ingredients:
- 1 (8-ounce) package tempeh, crumbled
- 1 tablespoon olive oil
- 1 teaspoon smoked paprika
- 1/2 teaspoon garlic powder
- 1/2 teaspoon ground cumin
- 1/4 teaspoon chipotle pepper powder
- 1/2 teaspoon salt
- 1/2 cup vegetable broth
- 2 cloves garlic, minced
- 2 tablespoons tomato paste
- 4 large lettuce leaves

Instructions:
1. In a large skillet, heat the olive oil over medium heat.
2. Add the crumbled tempeh and spices to the pan and stir until the tempeh is evenly coated and lightly browned.
3. In a separate small bowl, mix together the vegetable broth, garlic, and tomato paste.
4. Once the tempeh is lightly browned, reduce heat to low and pour the broth mixture into the pan. Stir until the tempeh is evenly coated in the sauce.
5. Simmer the tempeh for 8-10 minutes, stirring occasionally, until the sauce thickens.
6. Divide the tempeh among the lettuce leaves and serve.

Nutrition information: Serving size: 1 wrap; Calories: 146; Total Fat: 6 g; Saturated Fat: 1 g; Sodium: 48 mg; Carbohydrates: 12 g; Fiber: 2 g; Protein: 10 g.

97. BBQ Jackfruit Baked Potatoes

BBQ Jackfruit Baked Potatoes is a delicious vegan alternative for those who want to enjoy the smoky flavour of barbecue without consuming animal products. The vegan jackfruit meat is combined with potatoes to form a comforting and filling meal.

Serving: Makes 3-4 servings
Preparation Time: 10 minutes
Ready Time: 1 hour

Ingredients:
-2 large potatoes
-1 500g tin of jackfruit in brine
-1/4 cup of BBQ sauce
-2 tablespoons of olive oil
-Salt and pepper to season

Instructions:
1. Preheat oven to 400°F (200°C).
2. Wash the potatoes and poke them with a fork. Rub potatoes in olive oil and season with salt and pepper.
3. Place potatoes in oven and bake for 45 minutes.
4. Meanwhile, drain the jackfruit and pat dry using paper towels.
5. Heat a pan over high heat and add 1 tablespoon of olive oil.
6. Add jackfruit to pan and season with salt and pepper. Fry for 5 minutes or until it is slightly browned.
7. Reduce heat to medium-low, then add the BBQ sauce and fry for a further 5 minutes.
8. Take the potatoes out of the oven and slice open. Add a portion of the jackfruit to each potato and top with a sprinkle of cheese (optional).
9. Place in oven for a further 15 minutes until cheese is melted and potatoes are fully cooked.

Nutrition information: per serving:
Calories: 0
Protein: 0g
Fat: 0g
Carbohydrate: 0g

Fibre: 0g

98. Teriyaki Tofu Sushi Rolls

Try this delicious Teriyaki Tofu Sushi Rolls recipe for your next meal – perfect for weeknight dinners or impressive enough for entertaining.
Serving: 6
Preparation Time: 15 minutes
Ready Time: 45 minutes

Ingredients:
- 1/2 package of extra-firm tofu
- 3 tablespoons teriyaki sauce
- 1 tablespoon toasted sesame oil
- 2 tablespoons soy sauce
- 2 tablespoons honey
- 1 tablespoons cornstarch
- 6 sheets nori seaweed
- 2 cups cooked sushi rice
- 2 teaspoons sesame seeds

Instructions:
1. Preheat the oven to 375 degrees (F). Cut the tofu into thin cubes, and season with 1 tablespoon each of soy sauce, toasted sesame oil, and teriyaki sauce. Bake for 20 minutes.
2. In a small saucepan over medium heat, combine the remaining soy sauce, teriyaki sauce, honey, and cornstarch. Stir until the mixture thickens into a syrup-like texture, then remove from the heat and set aside.
3. Lay a sheet of nori on a piece of plastic wrap. Spread 1/6 of the cooked sushi rice along the middle of the nori, and sprinkle with sesame seeds. Arrange 1/6 of the tofu cubes on the rice.
4. Using the edge of the plastic wrap, roll the nori and rice around the tofu until a tight log is formed. Continue with the remaining Ingredients until all six rolls are formed.
5. Cut each roll into 8 equal pieces, drizzle with the teriyaki syrup, and serve.

Nutrition information: Per serving, the Teriyaki Tofu Sushi Rolls contain 286 calories, 7.6 g fat, 44.2 g carbohydrates, and 8.5 g protein.

99. Vegan "Beef" and Potato Curry

Vegan "Beef" and Potato Curry is a delicious vegan meal that will satisfy any appetite. Made with vegan beef crumbles, potatoes, and aromatic spices, this vegan curry is a flavorful and easy-to-make dish.
Serving: 4
Preparation time: 10 minutes
Ready time: 25 minutes

Ingredients:
-2 tablespoons vegetable oil
-1 onion, diced
-3-4 cloves garlic, minced
-8 ounces of "vegan beef" crumbles
-1-2 tablespoons of curry powder
-1 tablespoon of garam marsala
-1 teaspoon of turmeric
-1 teaspoon of ground coriander
-1 teaspoon of cumin
-1/2 teaspoon of cayenne pepper (or more to taste)
-4 potatoes, cubed
-1 can of coconut milk
-1 cup water
-1-2 tablespoons of maple syrup or coconut sugar
-Salt and pepper to taste

Instructions:
1. Heat the oil in a large pot over medium-high heat.
2. Add the onion and garlic and cook, stirring, until beginning to soften, about 2 minutes.
3. Add the "beef" crumbles and cook, stirring, for an additional 3 minutes.
4. Add the curry powder, garam marsala, turmeric, coriander, cumin, and cayenne+ pepper and stir to combine.

5. Add the potatoes, coconut milk, water, maple syrup (or coconut sugar), and salt and pepper to taste. Stir to combine.
6. Bring to a gentle boil, reduce heat to low, cover and simmer for 10-15 minutes, stirring occasionally, until potatoes are cooked through.
7. Taste and adjust seasonings to your preference.
8. Serve over rice or over cooked quinoa. Enjoy!

Nutrition information:
Calories: 250 per serving
Carbohydrates: 29 g
Protein: 8 g
Fat: 11 g
Fiber: 3 g
Sugar: 3 g
Sodium: 600 mg

100. Jackfruit BBQ Sliders

Get ready for a delicious and unique take on the classic BBQ slider with these Jackfruit BBQ Sliders! This vegan-friendly slider is made with homemade jackfruit instead of meat and is sure to be a hit for your next summer cookout.
Serving: Makes 6 to 8 sliders.
Preparation time: 25 minutes
Ready time: 45 minutes

Ingredients:
- 1 (20 ounce) can of young jackfruit in brine
- 2 cloves garlic, minced
- 2 tablespoons olive oil
- 1 tablespoon soy sauce
- 1 tablespoon tomato paste
- 2 teaspoons vegan Worcestershire sauce
- 1 teaspoon mustard powder
- ½ teaspoon paprika
- ½ teaspoon black pepper
- 6–8 mini slider buns or vegan dinner rolls
- Toppings of choice (lettuce, tomato, onion, vegan mayo, etc.)

Instructions:
1. Drain and rinse the jackfruit, then chop it into small pieces.
2. Heat the oil in a large skillet. Add the garlic and jackfruit and stir.
3. Stir in the soy sauce, tomato paste, Worcestershire sauce, mustard powder, paprika, and black pepper.
4. Cook the mixture for 5–7 minutes, stirring often until the jackfruit is golden brown.
5. Toast the slider buns, if desired.
6. Assemble the sliders by adding the jackfruit mixture and desired toppings.
7. Serve the sliders warm.

Nutrition information:
Calories: 111
Fat: 4 g
Carbohydrates: 14 g
Protein: 2 g

101. Tempeh Bacon and Spinach Salad

This Tempeh Bacon and Spinach Salad is a wholesome and easy-to-make side dish that's full of flavor. Enjoy a light and refreshing meal featuring savory, smoky tempeh bacon and fresh spinach.
Serving: Serves 2-3
Preparation time: 10 minutes
Ready time: 15 minutes

Ingredients:
- ¾ cup cubed tempeh bacon
- 4 cups fresh spinach
- ½ teaspoon garlic powder
- 2 tablespoons olive oil
- 2 tablespoons vinegar
- 2 tablespoons lemon juice
- 1 teaspoon Dijon mustard
- Salt and pepper to taste
- 1 garlic clove, minced

Instructions:
1. Preheat a large skillet over medium-high heat and add the cubed tempeh bacon. Cook for 5 minutes, stirring often, until the tempeh bacon is lightly browned.
2. In a large bowl, combine the spinach, garlic powder, olive oil, vinegar, lemon juice, and Dijon mustard. Stir until all Ingredients are evenly distributed.
3. Add the tempeh bacon to the spinach mixture and toss until combined.
4. Season with salt and pepper, to taste.
5. Serve the salad chilled or at room temperature.

Nutrition information: (Per Serving) Calories: 250; Total Fat: 15 g; Saturated Fat: 3 g; Monounsaturated Fat: 10 g; Cholesterol: 0 mg; Sodium: 246 mg; Carbohydrate: 16 g; Dietary Fiber: 4 g; Sugar: 2 g; Protein: 12 g

CONCLUSION

"The Green Butcher: 101 Meatless Recipes"

The Green Butcher: 101 Meatless Recipes is the perfect go-to cookbook for anyone looking to reduce their meat intake or cut out meat altogether. With over one hundred delicious and easy-to-follow recipes, there's something to satisfy every palate. Every dish is a flavorful and nutritious vegetarian or vegan meal that's sure to become a family favorite. The recipes, made with fresh ingredients, are perfect for a quick lunch, a creative dinner, or something to bring to a potluck or office party. The simple instructions make it easy to replicate dishes like slow cooker quinoa chili, pinto bean tacos, black bean burgers, veggie stir-fry, and veggie-loaded pizza.

Whether you are vegetarian, vegan or simply trying to reduce the amount of meat you consume, The Green Butcher will provide you with an essential resource. Not only will it provide an array of tasty and nutritious recipes to help you switch to a more plant-based diet, it also contains valuable information and tips for living an overall healthier life. Readers will gain an understanding of the health benefits of cutting back on meat, learn the importance of sourcing locally, find recipes for vegan and vegetarian meals, as well as some tips for making the most of a plant-based diet.

The Green Butcher is an invaluable resource for those looking to reduce their meat consumption and transition to a more plant-based lifestyle. Whether you're a novice or expert, this cookbook provides simple instructions and delicious recipes that are sure to tingle the taste buds while providing nutritious meals with wholesome ingredients. Begin your journey to a healthier you with The Green Butcher!